THE ENGLISH RESISTANCE

THE UNDERGROUND WAR AGAINST THE NORMANS

PETER REX

TEMPUS

To my wife Christina

*and also to my little dog Oscar, without whose
dedicated enthusiasm and encouragement this
book would have been finished weeks earlier!*

This edition first published 2006

Tempus Publishing Limited
The Mill, Brimscombe Port,
Stroud, Gloucestershire, GL5 2QG
www.tempus-publishing.com

© Peter Rex, 2004, 2006

The right of Peter Rex to be identified as the Author
of this work has been asserted in accordance with the
Copyrights, Designs and Patents Act 1988.

British Library Cataloguing in Publication Data.
A catalogue record for this book is available from the British Library.

ISBN 0 7524 3733 X
Typesetting and origination by Tempus Publishing Limited
Printed and bound in Great Britain

Contents

Foreword

England has become a residence for foreigners and the
property of strangers. At the present time there is no
English earl nor bishop nor abbot; foreigners all they prey
upon the riches and vitals of England.

William of Malmesbury, 1135

U ntil quite recently, little attention has been paid by
historians, blinded by the very fact of its success,
to the process, after Hastings, by which William
the Conqueror made good his claim to the English throne
against the will of the English. Much of the evidence for
opposition to the Norman regime has been dealt with
only cursorily, if at all. William the Conqueror's campaigns
against the rebels have usually been dealt with very briefly
and resistance has been summarily dismissed as ineffective,
largely because in the end, that resistance was overcome
in a singularly brutal manner. Even accounts which have
looked at the campaigns from a purely military standpoint
have failed to deal with the politics of the situation.

Having retained an interest in the Norman Conquest
ever since first studying it at Bristol under Professor David

Douglas in 1952, and stimulated by an interest in the career of Hereward the Outlaw, the defender of Ely, this book is written to go some way towards filling the gap by presenting an unfamiliar facet of a familiar story. In doing so I was struck by the curious parallels between the situation in England during the first five years of Norman rule and that of France under Nazi Germany during the Second World War.

For several years England was divided, like France, into an occupied and an unoccupied zone, the former governed directly by the new Norman lords with the assistance of quislings and collaborators, and the latter retained in the hands of its native landowners, most, but by no means all, of whom had submitted to the Norman king. Gradually, resistance grew and took shape, efforts were made to secure that assistance from overseas, notably from Denmark, or from Scotland, without which the Normans could never be expelled from the country. A guerrilla movement formed by 'Wildmen' (whom the Normans called *silvatici*) was organised with its bases in remote areas of forest and marsh, such as the North Yorkshire Hills and the Fens of East Anglia.

This book, therefore, deals with the identity of both those who led the Resistance and those who collaborated, since many of them will be unfamiliar to most readers. It deals with the warfare between the exiled Earl Tostig of Northumbria and his brother Harold Godwinson, and considers the effects of the battles of Fulford and Stamford Bridge in fatally weakening English resistance to the Norman Invasion. It then looks at all the campaigns of the Resistance from 1067 to 1071, examining the nature and motives of the Resistance Movement and the reasons for its successes and failures.

Attention then switches to the activities of the Lincolnshire thegn Hereward who led a last determined stand against King William in the Isle of Ely. His career and identity are examined, the attack on Peterborough Abbey and the defence and conquest of Ely are described and then followed by an account of how lands once held by Hereward before 1066 became part and parcel of the barony of Bourne in the twelfth century, leading to his adoption by the Wake family as their presumed ancestor. This book ends by looking at some of the evidence for a revival of English identity and history, which long antedated the Conquest, and shows how men began once more to claim pre-Conquest ancestry, rather as older Australian families now look back to their convict forebears.

The maps included are not intended to be cartographically accurate in every respect, they are intended only to clarify the locations mentioned in the text.

I have referred throughout to those who fought against the Normans as the English rather than as Anglo-Saxons because, as the sources show, that is what they called themselves. Until the coming of the Normans, the English lived in an England ruled by the King of England.

As many of the persons referred to in the text are rarely mentioned more than cursorily in standard general histories of the Conquest, a short note identifying the principal protagonists and collaborators can be found in chapter 11.

In writing this book I freely acknowledge the invaluable research carried out by such scholars as Elisabeth van Houts, Ann Williams, Cyril Hart, Marjorie Chibnall and many others whose works are listed in the bibliography and without whose labours this book could not have been written. The views expressed are, of course, entirely my own, as are any errors. I would like to thank, in particular, the Librarians of St John's College, Cambridge for granting access to their Library; Dr Janet Fairweather for allowing me to read vital sections of her, then unpublished (book pub. Woodbridge, September 2005), translation of the *Liber Eliensis*; my son Dr Richard Rex of Queen's College, Cambridge for his encouragement and support and my wife Christina for photographs, charts and sketch maps, as well as trenchant constructive criticism.

I

Three Battles
in One Year

Tostig, tyrant Earl of Northumbria, had ruled his earldom with a heavy hand since his appointment as Siward's successor. His draconian efforts to bring some conception of law and order to Northumbria provoked such widespread opposition that he needed a permanent bodyguard of 200 men. He had been an enthusiastic raiser of tolls and taxes and was frequently absent from his earldom at the court of King Edward the Confessor or on his lands in Northamptonshire, Bedfordshire and Huntingdon, leaving the conduct of government at home to his deputy Copsige. Copsige had the same disadvantage as his master, that he was neither from the House of Siward nor the House of Bamburgh (the hostile native rulers of the province).

In 1064 Tostig was accused by the Northumbrians of having 'despoiled of life and land all those over whom he could tyrannise', of robbing churches of their land and especially of procuring the deaths of the thegns Gamel son of Orm and Ulf son of Dolfin, key members of the opposition. 'Florence of Worcester' claims he had them 'treacherously slain in his own chamber', at York while they were under safe conduct. Tostig was also accused of complicity in the murder of Cospatrick, heir of the native Earls of Bernicia (between Hadrian's Wall and Bamburgh). Florence claims that he was 'treacherously slain' in the king's court on the orders of Queen Edith, Tostig's sister. Thus Tostig was attempting, in time-honoured fashion, to eliminate his opponents. Cospatrick was the youngest son of Earl Uhtred of the House of Bamburgh with a claim on the earldom and a supporter of King Edward in Cumberland. All three were related to each other as members of the highest Northumbrian aristocracy, descendants of Earl Waltheof I of Bamburgh.

The House of Bamburgh had been waiting for its chance and with Aethelwine, Bishop of Durham, formed an alliance with the priests of Durham against Tostig. Following the levy of a particularly heavy tax, and while Tostig was absent at court, some 200 Northumbrians, led by the thegns Gamalbeorn, Dunstan son of Athelnoth and Ghiniarain son of Heardulf, rose in rebellion, seized York, slew Tostig's household, his huscarls and 200 of his retainers, and declared the absentee earl an outlaw.

Continuing south through Mercia and ravaging Northamptonshire, where Tostig held many estates, they chose Morcar, brother of Edwin, Earl of Mercia, as their earl. He was a compromise candidate as Waltheof, the late Earl Siward's son, would have been unacceptable to the Northumbrians, and Oswulf son of Eadwulf was not acceptable to the Yorkshiremen. They collected troops from Lincolnshire, Nottinghamshire and Derbyshire, having, according to the *Vita Edwardi*, slaughtered Tostig's men at York and Lincoln and plundered the land, slaying men, burning houses and carrying off livestock. At Northampton they met Earl Harold, sent by the king at Tostig's request, to seek a compromise. There, supported by Earl Edwin and his Welsh allies, the Princes Bleddyn and Rhiwallon, they forced the king, through his chief adviser, Tostig's brother Harold, to confirm the outlawry and their choice of Morcar. The message was clear: dismiss Tostig or they would make war on King Edward. The Northumbrians had now won a similar role in the selection of an earl to that played by the Witan in the selection of a king. Tostig had no option but to accept exile and Morcar became earl. King Edward then sent Harold back to Northampton where, in the king's name, he 're-enacted there the laws of Cnut'. One source, admittedly late, the *De Northambrorum Comitibus* (about the Earls of Northumbria) claims that the North was to be administered by Edwin and Morcar jointly and that Oswulf son of Eadwulf (who later murdered Copsige), was given control of the area between the Tyne and the Tweed.

The revolt also achieved something else. It resulted in the forging of an alliance between the House of Bamburgh and the citizens of York. This was a great achievement which was to be repeated in 1068 until destroyed by the Conqueror. It also created a situation in which the rebels represented two out of the three great earldoms. This explains Harold Godwinson's unwillingness to take on both Northumbria and Mercia in defence of his brother Tostig who, with his wife Judith, sought refuge with his brother-in-law Count Baldwin of Flanders, who assigned him to be deputy commander of the garrison of St Omer. There he stayed for the winter of 1065. He was, therefore, absent when King Edward died and Earl Harold became king.

From Flanders, having raised a fleet of up to sixty ships, according to the *Anglo-Saxon Chronicle*, Earl Tostig went raiding in England, hoping that by doing so he could bring about his recall to power. Having raided the Isle of Wight and then approached Sandwich, he left hurriedly when he learnt that his brother, King Harold, was on his way with his own larger fleet. The outlawed earl then attempted a landing in force somewhere on the Humber, ravaging the province of Lindsey. Repulsed by Earl Edwin of Mercia and deserted by most of his shipmen, Tostig then fled north to Scotland, having now only twelve ships left, about 700 men.

One source says that he met Harald Hardrada, King of Norway, in Scotland, another that they met on the River Tyne as they had arranged the previous spring. Tostig had also been joined by his Northumbrian supporter Copsige, with seventeen ships, so that it all seems pre-arranged. Harald Hardrada had the reputation of being the foremost soldier of his age, having fought all over the East from the Bosphorus to Novgorod. He had commanded the Varangian Guard (a kind of foreign legion manned by Scandinavians) at Byzantium and married the sister of the Russian king. More recently, he had fought long wars with Swein Estrithson of Denmark and, having now made peace with him, was free to invade England.

GATE FULFORD

Harald had 300 ships carrying an invasion force of as many as 15,000 men. Known capacities of various Viking ships could range from twenty oars to sixty, a forty-oar ship being the commonest with the full complement for a ship ranging from fifty to eighty men, including non-rowers. The Norwegian force advanced on York, sweeping aside the northern army of about 4,000 to 5,000 men, at Gate Fulford, just south of York. Gate Fulford was a manor belonging to Morcar and had been selected as the rallying point for his forces and those of Earl Edwin of Mercia. The armies met along a ditch between the river and the fen and the earls lost more men by drowning than by battle. It is said there were so many corpses that the Norwegians could advance dryfoot over the fen. *The Saga of Harald Hardrada* quotes Stein Hardison:

> The gallant Harald drove along,
> Flying but fighting, the whole throng.
> At last, confused, they could not fight,
> And the whole body took to flight.
> Up from the river's silent stream
> At once rose desperate splash and scream;
> But they who stood like men this fray
> Round Morukari's body lay.

This defeat was the end of the earls' reputation for military ability and explains both their absence from Hastings and their reluctance to face Duke William in battle so soon afterwards. Their heavy losses deprived them of any chance of effective action during the critical weeks of October. Also present at the battle, unnoticed by the English Chroniclers, was Earl Waltheof, who led the survivors back to York. In the song called 'Harald's Stave' his men's desperate fight is recorded:

> Earl Waltheof's men
> Lay in the Fen
> By sword down hewed,
> So thickly strewed,
> That Norsemen say
> They paved a way
> Across the fen
> For the brave Norsemen.

STAMFORD BRIDGE

Meanwhile, all that summer, King Harold Godwinson awaited the arrival of Duke William's invasion force, 'because he had been told that William the Bastard meant to come here to conquer this country'. Eventually, as supplies of food began to run out, he had to allow the levies (called the 'fyrd') to go home and to disband most of his fleet. Some of the ships were wrecked by the weather while moving to London. News of Hardrada's preparations would have prompted some of the naval withdrawal. The Normans certainly knew of Hardrada's preparations. William of Poitiers talks of King Harold Godwinson laying a naval ambush with an armed fleet 'of up to 700 ships' (although seventy is more likely; royal fleets were quite small. King Edward 'and all the earls' opposed Earl Godwin in 1052 with only fifty ships.) The Normans would have been relieved to find their channel crossing unopposed. Choice of a suitable landing site would have been helped by the reports which reached Duke William through the Abbot of Fécamp. The abbey held land at Steyning in the Adour Valley and elsewhere in Sussex before the Conquest. The abbot gave William useful advance information from his knowledge of the local geography, thus acting as a sort of one-man Fifth Column. His motive perhaps lay in the fact that King Harold had seized Steyning, or did Harold seize the manor when he became aware of the monks' pro-Norman activities?

Through a network of spies and informants on the Continent and in the North, Harold heard of the activities of Duke William and of the presence of Hardrada and Tostig at Ricall on the Yorkshire Ouse. This site, nine miles from York at the confluence of the Ouse and the Wharfe, effectively bottled up Morcar's ships lying at Tadcaster.

When Harold left London to confront the first of his antagonists he could not yet have known of the defeat of the earls, for he arrived at Stamford Bridge on 25 September, five days after Fulford. Here, in a hard-fought battle, he overcame the Norwegian king, who, with Tostig, was slain there. Hardrada was struck in the throat by an arrow; 'The king whose name would ill-doers scare,

The gold-tipped arrow would not spare'. The remnants of their army filled only twenty-four ships because the Norsemen preferred death before dishonour.

The gallant men who saw him fall would take no quarter; one and all resolved to die with their beloved king, around his corpse in a corpse-ring.

Accounts of the battle from English sources are sparse and Norse sources are eerily reminiscent of an account of the Battle of Hastings transposed to Stamford Bridge. The *Heimskringla* speaks of cavalry attacking in small groups and wheeling away and of how serious a matter it was for the English to ride against the Norwegians. But it also claims that the English attacked the Norwegians by circling around them on horseback (like the attacks around Pioneers' wagon-trains) which, because the battle was fought on a plain, and despite the English not being known for an ability to mount cavalry charges, is quite possible. The Norwegians were attacked in the open without all their arms and armour, much of which had been left with their ships, some twelve miles away at Riccall. The *Heimskringla* says:

> Without hauberks do we go in array to receive blows from the brown blade. Helmets shine. I have not my hauberk. Our gear is down by the ships.

The English may have been able to ride down some groups of men who had not been able to join or who had left the shield wall. Harold's force obviously had many horsemen, unremarkable for an army which had been required to move from London to York in a matter of days. The confusion between accounts of the two battles could have arisen from the presence of Danes at Hastings, as is claimed by William of Poitiers.

As an army could only march about twenty-five miles a day at most, Harold is unlikely to have marched with his foot soldiers the whole way. He would have taken his elite household troops, the huscarls and the king's thegns and other horsemen, riding north along one of two routes, collecting men along the way who were within one or two days' march or ride of the route. He could have chosen either Ermine Street or Watling Street. The obvious way lay directly north from London to Lincoln, whereas the other route meant going by way of Leicester and Nottingham, forking towards Lincoln. Both routes then proceed to York. Men were thus summoned from the adjacent counties to join those he had brought with him from London and the South. It was the roads which made Harold's moves possible, and they were to be of the utmost usefulness to the Conqueror in subsequently putting down rebellions. The three 'Roman' roads, Watling Street, Ermine Street and the Fosseway, were all broad enough to allow sixteen horsemen to ride abreast. The bushes on each side were kept cut back to deter ambushes and men could travel remarkably quickly along them. Harold's movement, using horses, was probably around forty miles in a day.

Wace, prebendary of Bayeux, in his *Roman de Rou* written in the twelfth century about ninety years after Hastings, provides a list of the shires that provided men for Harold which shows those which were passed on the march north and probably even those which had to contribute to the second levy raised as he came south to confront Duke William. It reads:

> LONDON; Kent; Hertford; Essex; Surrey & Sussex; St Edmunds & Suffolk; Norwich & Norfolk; Canterbury and Stamford; Bedford; Huntingdon; Northampton; YORK Buckingham; Nottingham; Lindsey and Lincoln; Salisbury; Bath and Somerset; Gloucester; Worcester; Winchester and Hampshire; Berkshire.

It looks as though the second half, beginning at York, includes mainly levies which arrived too late for Stamford

but were in good time for Hastings. That some shires sent
men later than others explains why the *Chronicle* accounts
insist that William was able to surprise Harold 'before
his army was drawn up in battle array' or 'before all the
army had come' or even 'before a third of his army was
in order for fighting'. Certainly Wace has in the first half
of his list, counties which lie along the probable line of
Harold's march. The exception is Canterbury, which seems
out of place with Stamford, unless this is a misreading for
Cambridge which is otherwise not mentioned. (Compare
Cantabyrig and *Cantabrigensis*) Strikingly, most of western
Mercia is missing, which follows if Edwin was still nursing
his wounds; as is Northumbria, where support would have
tended to go to Tostig not Harold.

HASTINGS

Having defeated the Norwegians and raced south Harold
found himself confronted by Duke William's invasion
force laying waste the land around Dover and Hastings,
the area in which lay the estates of many men committed
to support the Godwinson family. The ravaging is graphi-
cally pictured in sections forty-seven and fifty-two of the
Bayeux Tapestry. Even Domesday Book notes that 'On his
(William's) very first arrival, the vill (of Dover) itself was
burned down'. Harold, elated by his crushing defeat of
Hardrada and enraged by the duke's harrying of his supporters, decided, against the advice of his brother Gyrth,
Earl of East Anglia, on an immediate battle. William was
also advised not to attempt to fight Harold; Robert fitz-
Wymarc, King Edward's Breton staller, warned the duke
that Harold had destroyed Tostig and Hardrada and 'huge
armies'. He told him that Harold had a 'strong and numerous force' and advised him to build fortifications and retire
behind them and not offer battle. This was ignored and
William of Poitiers probably includes it in his account

to demonstrate William's courage and military foresight. There has been much debate about the size of the armies involved at Hastings but a recently discovered clue comes from the Poitevin Chronicler of St Maixent writing *c.*1126 in a passage which describes Harold as 'pseudo King of the English'; he claims of Harold 'It is said that his army counted 14,000 men.' This is the best estimate of any Chronicler and it may be that this figure comes from the leader of the Poitevin contingent, Aimeri de Thouars, one of the ten men listed by William of Poitiers as having taken part in the battle.

The result, by no means a foregone conclusion at the outset, was defeat and death for Harold and his brothers and many thousands of their thegns. In a hard-fought and very bloody battle lasting most of the day, the English were finally defeated, not least because following the deaths earlier in the day of Gyrth and Leofwine, Harold himself was also struck down. With his death, the defeat of the English was accomplished. William of Malmesbury's verdict was mordant. He describes the English as 'engaging William more with rashness and precipitate fury than military skill' and says that 'they doomed themselves and their country to slavery by one, and that an easy, victory.'

The course of that battle has been described often and needs no repetition here. The battle between two contrasting styles of warfare was never a foregone conclusion but in the end, the Norman victory depended upon their heavy cavalry and their use of crossbowmen. The Norman *miles* (usually, but not always, meaning 'knight') was a *loricatus* or armoured man wearing helmet and mail coat (variously termed *byrnie* or *lorica*) and a carrying a shield. His arms were spear, sword and perhaps a mace. Facing the Normans were the English thegns and (from the Danish tradition) huscarls. They fought on foot and were similarly armoured with helmet and mail coat. Their shields differed from those of the Normans.

English shields protected a standing man and were either round or oblong and a line of men formed the famous shield-wall; the Normans on horseback used a kite-shaped shield. In addition to a sword the English used the dreaded two-handed battleaxe and preferred the throwing spear or javelin rather than the longer lance type used by the Normans. Men on both sides would be carrying 50lbs of iron, almost four stone.

The consequences of Hastings now concern us. The *Old English Chronicle* summarises as follows:

> But inasmuch as the English were drawn up in a narrow place, many retired from the ranks, and very few remained true to him; nevertheless, from the third hour of the day until dusk he bravely withstood the enemy, and fought so valiantly and stubbornly in his own defence, that the enemy's forces could hardly make any impression. At last, after great slaughter on both sides, about twilight the king, alas! fell. There were also slain Earl Gyrth and his brother, Earl Leofwine, and nearly all the nobility of England.

English casualties in the three battles of 1066 had been catastrophic. Unknown numbers died in each battle and no estimate is possible. What can be done is to trace, in the pages of Domesday Book and in scattered references in chronicles and charters, the names of a few handful of men who can be said with certainty to have died or to have been driven into exile by Norman hostility and the loss of their lands. There are no recorded names of anyone who died at Gate Fulford.

For Stamford Bridge we know of the deaths of Hardrada and Tostig, from Kent came Abbot Aethelwig's uncle who leased Witton from his nephew, and 'died subsequently in Harold's battle against the Northmen', and two of Harold's thegns from Essex and Worcestershire. Apart from these, the identifiable casualties are from Hastings.

The list is not a long one. It begins with Harold himself and his brothers Gyrth and Leofwine and it is noticeable that most of the other available names come from the earldoms of these men. They come from Berkshire and Hampshire, including the Abbot of New Minster at Winchester and twelve of his monks, from Bedfordshire, Essex, Huntingdon, Cambridgeshire, Norfolk and Suffolk and Lincolnshire. Many of these shires lie along the route of Harold's marches, which suggests that these suffered the most casualties.

Finally, there is a writ addressed to Abbot Baldwin of Bury St Edmunds from William, commanding him to surrender the lands of men in St Edmunds' soke 'who stood against me in battle and were slain there'. The exact number of these men cannot be ascertained, but the writ reveals the conqueror's policy, confiscation of the estates of anyone who had fought against him which included sokemen (freemen holding their own land but under the jurisdiction of a lord) as well as thegns.

It is hardly coincidental that the areas from which these men came were the earliest to submit to the Normans, being now without potential leaders. It was to be some years before eastern England dared to oppose William. East Anglia was given to Ralph the Staller, one of King Edward's household officers and of Breton origin, as a replacement for Gyrth. He had lands in Norfolk and was probably appointed shortly after William's coronation, in line with that king's proclaimed policy of ruling as the legitimate successor of Edward the Confessor. William was careful to ensure that as far as possible Harold's reign was written out of the record and that he should not be referred to as 'king'. As the Domesday Book shows, with its constant reference back to the 'Time of King Edward', William set out from the beginning to backdate his reign so that it commenced 'on the day King Edward was alive and dead'. The effect of this was to make all those who fought against him, especially at Hastings, into rebels whose lands could then be confiscated. He promised to guarantee the lands and offices of those who submitted promptly, yet he also had to reward his followers who expected to be enriched with the lands of the conquered.

THE OCCUPATION BEGINS

There was an ominous and doubtful time, between the Battle of Hastings and the coronation at Christmas 1066, when it remained uncertain whether the English nobles who had survived the war would in fact submit. There was a real possibility that the Danelaw magnates would refuse to accept the Battle of Hastings as decisive. They might invite Swein Estrithson of Denmark to assert his claim to the English throne. There is evidence that some of the other leading men might well have been prepared to make Edgar the Aetheling king but apparently his foreign birth was against him as was his youth. He also lacked any ties of kinship with the nobility which might have encouraged a solid party of supporters to emerge. Nonetheless, Hastings would have appeared less decisive at that time than it seems to us now and the death of the English king did not lead to immediate submission. The *Anglo-Saxon Chronicle* says that Ealdred, Archbishop of York, and the citizens of London wanted Edgar for king 'as was his proper due by birth'.

Earls Edwin and Morcar seemed at first inclined to support him and we have the strange act of Abbot Brand of Peterborough who, chosen by the monks to succeed Abbot Leofric, sought confirmation in office from Edgar 'because the local people expected that he would be king' and the Aetheling 'gladly gave assent to it', thus playing the part expected of a king. William's anger when he heard of this suggests that support for Edgar was more widespread than is apparent now. In the event the nobles dithered. The *Chronicle* says that the earls promised to fight for Edgar but 'always the more it ought to have been forward, the more it got behind.'

After the battle William made ready to accept submissions and in order to induce the men of the South-East to surrender he made a savage assault on Romney. The *Chronicle* says he permitted his men to keep on burning the villages and slaying the natives. He 'inflicted such punishment as he thought fit for the slaughter of his men who had landed there by mistake' at Romney because they had been 'attacked and scattered with great loss by the fierce people of the region' says William of Poitiers. As a result, Dover, 'terror-stricken at his approach… lost all confidence in the natural defences and fortifications of the place and the multitude of men'. The garrison got ready to surrender and did so all the more rapidly when the squires set fire to their 'castle' (which probably means the wooden palisade around the fort). Canterbury then surrendered of its own accord and the people swore fealty and gave hostages as 'the mighty metropolitan city shook with terror' for fear of total ruin if it resisted further and hastened to secure its status as the city of the archbishop.

In London Archbishop Stigand (according to William of Poitiers, but probably actually Ealdred), along with 'the sons of Aelfgar and other nobles', was threatening battle and had chosen Edgar the Aetheling as king. 'Their highest wish was to have no lord who was not a compatriot'. But we are also contrarily told that the bishops in particular gave no support to Edgar. Continued resistance to William was, then, briefly considered by the remnants of the Witan supported by the citizens of London who formed a faction which wanted to make Edgar the Aetheling king. It was troops belonging to Edgar, provided no doubt by these supporters, that skirmished with the Normans and caused William to forego the idea of taking the city by force of arms.

William played a calculated waiting game, marching in a wide circle around London and cutting the city off from its hinterland to the west and north upon which it depended for both food and income. While this was done the town of Winchester, site of the Treasury, at the instigation of Edward's widow Queen Edith, sent gifts and promise of submission. Guy of Amiens says bitterly that the citizens there 'flocked to submit... like flies to a running sore.' Other towns followed suit. The duke had been deterred from an immediate attack on London by the skirmish between the citizens and a force of 500 knights. London troops, said to be Edgar's men, had made the sortie but were forced to retreat, shamefully according to Poitiers, yet they had driven back the advance guard, with heavy losses on the Norman side, which had failed to take London Bridge. William of Poitiers insists that the citizens of London could themselves supply 'a numerous and formidable force' and he further explains that 'they had now been joined by so many troops that they could hardly be housed even in this large town'; yet London was unable to withstand William's blockade. After the skirmish, fire added to the carnage as all the houses on the Southwark side of the river were torched. Significantly, William made no further attempt to fight his way across London Bridge. Instead he made his way via Surrey, northern Hampshire and Berkshire by ford and bridge to Wallingford. He then moved towards London through Buckinghamshire and Bedfordshire to Berkhamstead. Archbishop Stigand had made his submission at Wallingford, influenced no doubt by the surrender of Canterbury and his consequent loss of control over its lands and revenues, confirming his fealty by oath. The churchmen, especially the bishops, concerned also about their lands, preferred a strong king who could guarantee them their integrity of title and possession. Some of the earliest writs of the Conqueror are confirmations of ecclesiastical estates. The churches secured their endowments by a combination of submission, gifts to William, and a readiness to accept Norman knights as tenants on their lands.

In London opinions remained divided, with Archbishop Ealdred, the citizens and the shipmen favouring Edgar for king. We are told that 'no one meant to come to him' (that is, William) and that was why he had gone 'inland with all his army that was left to him and that came to him afterwards from overseas' (one of the few references to reinforcements after Hastings) and then that the prominent men submitted 'out of necessity'. William preferred economy of effort, avoiding any pitched battle and preferring the blockade. He occupied the surrounding countryside and waited, depriving the Londoners of food and revenue – tactics successfully used later in the north of England. It was at this time that he addressed writs to all the thegns of Staffordshire, Worcestershire and Gloucestershire, in the expectation that they would obey, and they did so.

In the end, the remaining leadership in London caved in. The chief men of the city, submitting to William, offered hostages, probably at Berkhamstead after the ravaging of Middlesex and Hertfordshire where they 'sought pardon for any hostility they had shown him and surrendered themselves and all their property to his mercy' and the king 'restored all their possessions and treated them with great honour' (Poitiers). This was accomplished by the 'Peace Party' of appeasers, led by foreign-born bishops from Normandy and Lorraine who preferred discreet submission to open revolt. A Writ issued later by William, as king, addressed to Bishop William, Gosfrith the Portreeve and all the Burgesses of London, French and English, confirms his conciliatory approach to London. It preserves their rights and property and commands them to observe the laws of King Edward. It is the letter of a foreign king aware that his rule is not yet safe, especially if the men of his greatest city are disaffected. In due course other town burgesses were to seek to secure their municipal customs; the lawmen at Lincoln and Stamford; the judges at York and Chester; as well as the folkmoot and hustings at London and Southwell.

Others, including Copsige, are said to have submitted after the coronation, at Barking, where William stayed while the Tower was being built in London. William of Poitiers, while insisting that opposition was now so remote that William could go hawking and hunting, has to admit that he awaited the building of castles in London, 'against the inconstancy of the numerous and hostile inhabitants', which explains his sojourn at Barking as he was unwilling to enter London until its inhabitants had been suitably overawed, 'for he saw that it was of the first importance to contain the Londoners strictly.'

Edwin and Morcar had gone to their lands in Mercia, which had so far been unaffected by the war, and after Berkhamstead, seem to have either renewed their submission at Barking or delayed it until then, having submitted by proxy earlier. Then the Aetheling Edgar, who, according to Orderic, 'had been proclaimed king by the English, also hesitated to take up arms and humbly submitted himself and the kingdom to William' who 'treated him as long as he lived like one of his own sons'. Others who submitted include Bishop Wulfstan of Worcester, Walter, Bishop of Hereford, the leading citizens of London and Esgar the Staller, Sheriff of Middlesex. To these can be added Edgar the Aetheling and Ealdred the Archbishop of York, along with Siward son of Athelgar and his brother Ealdred (cousins of Eadric the Wild from Shropshire) and another West Midlands thegn 'Thorkell of Limis' (who may well be the thegn of Arden in Warwickshire). Esgar seems to have made a deal, that he would submit if promised continuation in office. If so, it was to no avail; he was in fact replaced. The *Carmen de Hastinge Proelio* has a curious story that William intended originally to bombard London with siege engines, but that 'Ansgard' (usually identified as Esgar the Staller), described as being in charge of the defences, negotiated surrender, hoping to trick William, but was himself deceived by being replaced. The *Carmen* attempts retrospectively to show a last despairing effort by the English to defy the Conqueror, an eleventh-century version of 'London can take it'. The author also supports the view that Edgar had been chosen as king. As Orderic concludes:

> So by the grace of God England was subdued within the space of three months and all the bishops and nobles of the realm made their peace with William, begging him to accept the crown according to English custom.

Both William of Jumièges and William of Poitiers offer contrasting accounts of William's blockade. In Poitiers, as in the *Chronicles*, the leaders went to parley with William, and submit. In Jumièges the skirmish between the Normans and Edgar's men takes place in the main square of the city (*in platea urbis*) and is then repelled, with submission following. The *Waltham Chronicle* remarks coldly that the Londoners were 'accustomed to obey a king and wished to have a king as their lord'.

Others who must have submitted, at either Berkhamstead or Barking, include the Stallers Bondi and Eadnoth, Aethelwig, Abbot of Evesham, who proved to be a firm supporter of King William, most of the sheriffs and all bar one of the bishops (several of whom were of foreign birth or educated on the Continent). All sources agree that the leading magnates made a submission to William. The *Worcester Chronicle* says 'they submitted out of necessity after most damage had been done... and gave him hostages and swore oaths to him' and that he in turn promised to be a gracious liege lord to them. The *Peterborough Chronicle* says only that after the coronation they paid taxes to him, gave him hostages and bought (or redeemed) their lands from him. Florence of Worcester, basing his account on a version of the *Chronicle* not now extant, says they surrendered and swore fealty (that is, loyalty and obedience) to him. Only of the peace made in 1072 by Malcolm, King of Scots, does the *Chronicle* say that he became William's vassal. On the other hand, the same word, 'submitted', is used of Tostig's acceptance of Harold Hardrada in 1066. Yet at Salisbury in 1086, where the *Chronicle* has all the land-holding men who were of any account bow to William and swear oaths of fealty (that is hold-oaths) to him, Florence of Worcester simply says they had to swear fealty, or fidelity, to him. Orderic has the fullest version:

> Renouncing allegiance to Edgar they made peace with William, acknowledging him as their lord and were graciously taken under his protection and reinvested with all their former offices and honours. The Londoners also took the wise course and surrendered to the duke, bringing him all the hostages he named and required.

The question is what the English thought they were doing when they made ceremonial submission to William and whether it differed from what William thought they were doing. The English were accustomed to accept a superior as their lord by the ceremony of 'commendation' in which a man on bended knee 'bowed' his head to his lord and swore a hold-oath, a promise 'to shun all that he shuns and love all that he loves… on condition that he keep me as I am willing to deserve and all that fulfil that our agreement was when I to him submitted and chose his will'. Domesday Book constantly states that one person was in this way the 'man' of another who was his lord. But there is no sign of investiture with land (a fief), only the bowing and oath taking, and commendation did not give the lord rights over his man's land, only over the man. This is not a ceremony appropriate to a class of barons or knights. It is not feudal 'homage' in which one man places his hands between those of another who is to be his lord and swears to become his vassal and is endowed with an estate. In justification of the English renunciation of allegiance, as in the rebellions, it must be recognised that a man who had 'submitted' to a lord could denounce the contract binding him to his lord if the lord wilfully abused his power over him. The lord had a general duty to keep faith with his vassal and not to act in such a way as to injure his life, honour and property. Florence of Worcester speaks of William making a 'treaty' with those who surrendered, that is making a bargain with them.

The Normans saw their 'homage' in the English ceremony of commendation and saw the hold-oath as an oath of fealty. William no doubt thought that they were becoming his vassals and that they were surrendering everything to him including lands and honours or offices, which he then, as the *Anglo-Saxon Chronicle* explicitly states, expected them to buy back from him. But did the earls and bishops and other officials realise what the Normans assumed they were doing? As William saw them as his vassals, he would, in his own judgement, be fully justified in treating them, when they opposed him, as rebellious vassals who then forfeited lands and honours to their lord. These could be re-granted to them, at a price, if they made their peace with him and were received back into his favour.

The English saw themselves as placing themselves under William's protection, taking him as their lord in the English manner, by bowing to him and swearing loyalty to him. Everywhere he went, we are told, men 'laid down their arms' and flocked to submit or negotiate surrender. The Aetheling Edgar was said to have received ample lands, though we have no account of their extent. 'Very many Englishmen (that is, those prepared to collaborate) received through his generous gifts what they had not received from their kinsmen or previous lords.' Others would have been angry when they realised that he expected them to redeem their lands from him for money. Perhaps in this fundamental misunderstanding the disillusionment leading to rebellion takes its roots. It is a misunderstanding from which King William profited enormously and it does perhaps lie further back in another oath-taking ceremony in Normandy.

According to William of Poitiers, Harold Godwinson, while he was William's unwitting 'honoured guest' in Normandy,

> swore fealty to the Duke employing the sacred ritual recog-
> nised among Christian men... took an oath of his own free
> will... that he would be the representative of the Duke at the
> court of his lord, King Edward, as long as the king lived...
> [and]... employ all his influence and wealth to ensure that
> after the death of King Edward the kingdom of England
> should be confirmed in the possession of the Duke... the
> Duke on his part who before the oath was taken had received
> ceremonial homage from him, confirmed to him at his request
> all his lands and dignities.

That is the Norman version of what happened, though the writer was not necessarily present. Several things can be said about this affair in the light of 'commendation'. Harold, effectively a prisoner in the duke's hands, was not a free agent. To gain his release he swore an oath, probably along the lines indicated by William of Poitiers, and gave hostages. In his own eyes, Harold had commended himself to the duke, bowing to him and swearing fealty to him under unspoken duress. The rest may well be a gloss put upon what happened by the Normans. The propaganda value of the oath lay not in the specific promises Poitiers alleges were made, but in the fact that William was later able to portray Harold as a perjurer and a rebellious vassal who had forfeited his lands and honours. This is shown by William's prompt confiscation of Harold's estates and those of his men, regarded as the vassals of the rebel vassal. In fact, as Harold was at that time William's prisoner, no oath sworn under duress could have

been binding upon him. It makes an interesting reference point for understanding the roots of the conflict between William and the English aristocracy after 1066. The fact all is not what it seems is indicated by the account in William of Poitiers, expressed through the words of a monk acting as go-between between the duke and King Harold before Hastings. This set piece allows William of Poitiers to put the case for William's claim to the throne yet again. Harold is made to admit that he had given William surety when in Normandy and the account includes the usual Norman claims, but Harold is permitted a defence, that the kingdom is his 'by right of gift of the same king, his lord' made by King Edward on his deathbed (which was considered binding under Anglo-Saxon law). The debate ends with the assertion that God would decide between them. It is worth noting that Norman accounts of Harold's sojourn in Normandy fit ill with the view of him given in the *Vita Edwardi*, of how he passed through various countries on his return from Rome by God's grace passing with watchful mockery through all ambushes as was his way.

Initially William gave every appearance of making a serious attempt to rule as King Edward's heir, making use of men who had held high office in Edward's reign. Edwin and Morcar, and Siward's heir Waltheof as well as Archbishops Stigand and Ealdred signed charters along-side Norman magnates like Odo of Bayeux, Geoffrey of Coutances, William fitzOsbern and Robert, Count of Mortain. Even in the ranks of lower officials the 'stall-ers' Bondi and Eadnoth attested charters. Eadnoth was to die leading the Somerset militia against Harold's sons in 1068. William also retained English sheriffs and the shires remained in English hands at least until 1069. There is also the case of Aethelwig, Abbot of Evesham, who held the authority of a Royal Justice over seven shires.

Yet the English position after Hastings was in theory, or potentially still, a strong one. Hastings probably seemed less decisive in 1066 than it now seems to us with hindsight and did not result in immediate and complete submission. The Earls Edwin and Morcar had not been involved in Harold's defeat. London, a city of great size for the time, with a population of 20,000 to 30,000, could have been held and the ships of the remains of Harold's and Morcar's fleets could have blockaded William while a second army was raised from shires not yet affected by the war and which had not yet even seen the Norman army. England remained in a state of suppressed rebellion. What was lacking was unity of purpose, determination to resist and any real agreement to unite behind an English king.

COLLABORATION AND SUBMISSION

Instead a party was formed led by Ealdred, Archbishop of York, and Wulfstan, Bishop of Worcester and recruited from all classes, which favoured accepting William as king. There is an eerie parallel between the Norman occupation of England and that of the German occupation of the Normans' country of origin in 1940. William of Normandy governed large areas of his new realm through what we might today call collaborators, even quislings.

It has been argued that the responsible leaders of English opinion recognised a plain truth, that there was no native claimant to the throne round whom they could rally. It is also argued that Edgar was incompetent and that his claim had already been rejected once when Harold had become king and therefore these leading men turned to the only candidate left, William, to make the best of a bad job. Yet, on the death of Edward the Confessor, Harold had acted decisively to seize the throne, making no attempt even to consider the claims of the Aetheling, who was only a boy. He had been not so much rejected as ignored. At that time he had had no party to support him. William also, like Harold, obtained the co-operation of the leaders

of the English Church. They had previously supported
Harold and had made no contact with William before
the battle, some even sent contingents of men to fight
in it, but now they were ready to serve the Conqueror.
Of the bishops, only Aethelwine of Durham is known to
have joined a rebellion against him. Archbishop Ealdred
of York and Wulfstan of Worcester placed all their years of
experience at his disposal and even Stigand of Canterbury
was made use of until the Papal Legate arrived to depose
him. These prelates expected William to seek their aid and
advice, yet he was to rob their churches for the benefit of
Normandy. In the first three years of the reign only one
Norman bishop was appointed, Remigius of Fécamp to
the see of Dorchester. But four Sees were held by men of
foreign birth, William of London, Herman of Sherborne,
Giso of Wells and Walter of Hereford, and one, Leofric of
Exeter, had been educated abroad.

It might not be too much to suggest that they formed a
fifth column, especially as foreign clergy favoured 'reform'
of the Church along continental lines. As for the monasteries, the earliest record of a replacement of an English abbot
by a Norman is the appointment of Thoroldr (or Turold)
to Malmesbury which, as he was moved to Peterborough
in 1069 on the death of Abbot Brand, must have taken
place shortly after the Conquest. Otherwise the monasteries remained in English hands until Lanfranc began his
programme of reform, beginning with the synod of 1072.
Yet it is clear that the monasteries did not entirely escape
William's attentions. They were suspected of harbouring
dissidents such as Bishop Aethelric, formerly of Durham,
who in 1069 was arrested and taken from his refuge at
Peterborough, and his brother, Bishop Aethelwine of
Durham who was outlawed.

The latter had been alarmed by William's northern
campaign and had fled to Scotland at the king's approach,
taking with him the relics of St Cuthbert. Aethelric seems

to have been held guilty by association. According to the Chroniclers it was Aethelwine who was to be one of the leaders of the revolt at Ely. The Chronicler insists that it was William's own action which triggered the attack on Peterborough which led to the siege of Ely. He says that 'the king had all the monasteries in England plundered' (under the year 1071 which is actually 1070). These events, the arrest and outlawry and the plundering of the monasteries are recorded as occurring at Easter that year. There then follows the account of the appointment of Thoroldr to Peterborough and all that flowed from that.

Government was continued on English lines, assisted by the staff of Edward's Household who carried on their work for William as they had for his predecessors, collecting *gelds*, dealing with sheriffs, issuing writs (still at this time in Old English). The Normans occupied the South-East and southern England, along with East Anglia where Ralph the Staller was made earl and a castle was built at Norwich. William's right-hand man, William fitzOsbern, had responsibility for the whole of this 'occupied zone', and was particularly to watch over the Welsh border. A large area of the west was under an Englishman, Aethelwig, Abbot of Evesham, but Devon and Cornwall were still untouched and the rest of the country north of a line from Bristol to The Wash had not yet seen a Norman. Areas the invader's hand had not yet touched might be left more or less to themselves until the government of the South and east had been placed on a secure footing. In the end the rebellions were to make William moderate his harshness towards the churches as he needed their support, and with it he managed to survive the revolts. But it is still true to say that everywhere William went collaboration became occupation.

2

The Occupation of Southern England

After the submissions came the coronation. The indefatigable spin doctor, William of Poitiers, maintains that William was in no hurry to be crowned and only agreed at Archbishop Ealdred's insistence. He claims that the situation was still confused, with rebels lurking around (already, in November 1066!) to 'disturb the tranquillity of the Kingdom' and William desired to have Matilda crowned at the same time, so emphasising his need to be cautious so near the summit of his ambitions, to become a king. He might have been testing the reaction of his followers to such an idea or merely showing the conventional reluctance to accept elevation to so high a rank so as not to appear too eager. In the event the army made up his mind for him and, led by the Viscount

Aimeri de Thouars, leader of the contingent from Poitou in Aquitaine, insisted that he accept the crown. The bishops also urged it upon him, especially Archbishop Ealdred. From the English standpoint it was vital. Once crowned he could take advantage of the customary rule that being crowned made him eligible to receive the hold-oaths of all free men. It was probably immediately after the coronation that, having taken the oaths from them, he was able to return the thegns' lands to them, at a price and conditionally. This would have been done in shire and hundred court before the king's officers.

The coronation itself passed smoothly enough except for the moment of Acclamation. Guards had been posted to prevent any treachery or disorder, but, according to Orderic, as a portent of future disasters, at the moment the assembled dignitaries cried out in acclamation of the new king, 'the armed guard outside imagined that some treachery was afoot (and) set fire to some buildings'; panic ensued and everyone present fled, leaving the new king alone and trembling, whether with fear or rage is not stated. The real sting is in Orderic's concluding remark,

> The English, after hearing of the perpetration of such misdeeds, never again trusted the Normans, who seemed to have betrayed them, but nursed their anger and bided their time to take revenge.

William was now an anointed king and able to claim the full range of royal powers. He had been anointed with Holy Oil, which added force to his claim that he had received the kingdom by the gift of God. In the eleventh century royal coronation seemed almost to be on the verge of being recognised as an eighth sacrament of the Church and the idea of the 'priest-king' is a Norman motif. This aura of ecclesiastical blessing contributed to the consolidation of William's power in the early years of the reign, allowing him to claim the loyalty inherent in the English concept of kingship. He was now the legitimate sovereign and consecrated holder of royal rights. He could tax the whole of England and his writ ran in every shire. He was, indeed, more truly a king than was the King of France. His avowed aim was to rule as the heir of Edward the Confessor and to this end he made, during his first four years, some attempt to rule with Englishmen in positions of authority, although we do not know to what extent this was acceptable to his Norman companions nor how long William intended to go on doing so. In practice, only Odo of Bayeux, who was eventually made Earl of Kent, and William fitzOsbern, soon to be Earl of Hereford, were given real governmental authority, acting with viceregal powers during William's absences in Normandy. The other Normans had to be satisfied with lands rather than honours and found that no surviving English earl had as yet lost his earldom.

William's aim was to secure the loyalty of the English as rightful heir of the Confessor. This was essential if he was ever to be able to reduce his dependence on the army. So the surviving earls, Edwin, Morcar and Waltheof, acted as members of the King's Council and witnessed his charters. The Archbishop of Canterbury, Stigand, was also involved until his deposition. He had replaced Archbishop Robert of Jumièges after he fled the country back in 1052 following the restoration of Earl Godwin, but had failed to obtain a pallium from Rome because of his uncanonical intrusion into the archbishopric (while the former archbishop still lived). He was also a pluralist, holding the See of Winchester as well as that of Canterbury. He was not removed from office until 1070 as William found it politic to have his support and advice, just as he found it convenient to have the assistance of the household officials and the sheriffs, useful tools of government who spoke and wrote English.

The archbishops, bishops and abbots retained their Sees and abbacies and, after making due submission, had their possession of Church lands confirmed. (The long lists of Church lands at the beginning of each county described in Domesday Book bear witness to the churchmen's success in retention.) Having submitted, they served William faithfully (as they had served both Edward and Harold). They submitted the more readily because William was able to claim papal backing for his invasion. Alexander II had sent him a consecrated banner to carry into battle and blessed the enterprise so that Harold, depicted as a perjurer (in his absence) and Archbishop Stigand, seen as schismatic, might be removed. So the bishops were complaisant and felt justified in their collaboration with the new regime. They proceeded to use their local influence to ensure the obedience of their flocks to the new government and their example was followed by the stallers, sheriffs and leading thegns. There was, therefore, very little spontaneous rebellion in what may, without exaggeration, be termed the 'occupied zone'. Orderic bears witness that some churchmen were 'covetous of high office' and therefore, he says, they 'shamelessly pandered to the king' to get bishoprics and abbacies, provostships, archdeaconries and deaneries. Several of them were eager for the English Church to embrace the Cluniac reform emanating from the Papacy and from continental monasteries. Only one bishop, Aethelwine of Durham, is known to have been involved in rebellion while his archbishop, Ealdred of York, placed his expertise and experience at the disposal of the new king, even performing his coronation.

The lay lords and landowners who made submission were allowed to retain their estates and offices, at least for a time. It was made very clear that the price of continued possession was acceptance of William's claim to be the rightful king. Yet the English seem not to have fully acquiesced in William's rule when William of Poitiers refers to 'a spirit of sullen rebellion'. Not all thegns would have been prepared to accept 'William the Bastard' as king. There was a long-standing tradition in England opposed to having bastard kings which ran all the way back to the Council of Chelsea in AD 787. This Legatine provincial synod laid down that only legitimate kings were to be chosen by the 'bishops and elders of the people' and none resulting from 'adulterous or incestuous procreation' (Cap. 12). Also it must be said that he had won the throne over the dead bodies of Anglo-Saxon thegns. That is why the claim had to be made that William was king by hereditary right and by the grant of God. One charter, of 1067, for the Abbey of Jumièges, calls William 'King (Basileus) of the Fatherland of the English by hereditary right' and his confirmation in 1066 of Abbot Brand's ownership of certain estates says he was 'King of the English by the Grant of God'.

It was useful for William to be able to claim that he was the legal heir of the Confessor, and a consecrated king, so that the new Norman lords had not only the rights but also the obligations of their English predecessors. Thus abbeys might recover lands after the death of the new Norman lord by showing that the land was loan land leased to a thegn for three lives and that the death marked the end of the third life. So usually a Norman was granted all the lands held by the thegn or thegns from whom his lands had been taken wherever they might be. Geoffrey Alselin received from the king the hall at Lincoln and all the lands in several shires previously held by Toki son of Outi. This man was one of those 'with sake and soke and toll and team in Lincolnshire', that is he had wide rights of jurisdiction in matters in dispute and to collect tolls. These rights imply a right to hold a manorial court. Geoffrey also received the lands of Ulf son of Tope who was probably Toki's nephew. By contrast, Roger de Busli had to amass his estates from the lands of more than eighty Englishmen from earls to minor thegns. It is this process of confiscation which caused Orderic to exclaim that 'England deprived of lawful heirs fell under the sway of foreign invaders led by the conquering William.'

Yet it was actually Harold's government that William took over, not Edward's. Harold had kept the secretariat, issued charters and minted coins all over England (more from his nine months have survived than from the reigns of Harold Harefoot and Harthacnut together). William, like Harold, was crowned at Westminster not Winchester. Use was made of English officials. For instance Regenbald, once Edward's priest in charge of his writing office, now became William's chancellor, in fact if not in title. A writ for Regenbald issued by King William is modelled on one from the Confessor, so it is likely that the new chancellor drafted it for himself. It grants him land in Latton and Eisey in Wiltshire 'as freely as it belonged to King Harald' (a rare recognition of Harold's status and, significantly, from the hand of an English official) and is addressed first to Eustace of Boulogne and then to other English office holders, and the bishops, Herman and Wulfstan, the stallers, Eadric and Brihtric and 'all the king's thegns in Wiltshire and Gloucestershire'. Addressed as it was to English authorities, it was issued before Norman administration had been set up in Wiltshire and dates to 1067.

Despite the apparent effort to involve Englishmen in his government, changes in the membership and character of the upper ranks of society became both inevitable and inexorable. The fate of the Old English aristocracy was catastrophic downfall. This was not only because they were the defeated survivors of what would prove a lost cause, in a precarious position dependent on royal favour which deteriorated rapidly and in the end became untenable, but also because of the heavy toll exacted by the three battles of 1066. No member of the House of Godwin was permitted to remain in authority or to retain much land and the earldom of Wessex disappeared completely.

The remaining English earls quickly disappeared from the scene, becoming ever more deeply involved in rebellion. At the same time, or earlier, the 200 or so king's thegns fell in battle and some 2,000 thegns of middle rank. They were, therefore, replaced by a dominant foreign aristocracy headed by about 180 major barons established on the recently conquered land in a manner which enhanced William's royal authority. Englishmen were eliminated almost entirely from the front rank of Anglo-Norman Society. By 1086 in all England south of the Tees there were only three Englishmen with estates of baronial extent and these were the three collaborators; Edward of Salisbury (whose descendants were to become earls) with 312 hides of land; Thorkell of Arden, son of Sheriff Aethelwine of Warwickshire, with 132 hides; and Colswein of Lincoln, who was possibly Town Reeve, with 100 hides. In the farther north Cospatrick son of Arnkell of Bamburgh had 145 carucates.

The real purpose of William's claim to be the legal successor of King Edward was to control the distribution of lands by means of a declared respect for English precedent. This helped to prevent the disorder which might otherwise have arisen from a free-for-all land grab. Compact blocks of estates were given to a select number of William's most committed supporters, men like Odo of Bayeux, the Counts of Eu and Mortain, William fitzOsbern and the Warenne and Montgomery families. Earldoms were given to some of these men and to collaborators like Ralph of Gael who was given East Anglia very early in the reign. This is evidence that he had submitted very soon after Hastings.

The office of sheriff became more important than 'shire-reeve' had been. They were now more like Norman vicomtes. These latter were ducal officials independent of the local count and themselves lesser magnates. They, rather than the count, governed the *comitatus* and this word was now used in England for 'shire'. Sheriffs in England were termed *vicecomes* in Latin. Old English sheriffs were appointed royal officials. They were responsible for the collection of the Old English land tax, the *geld*, which could be collected at need. They were easily removable and subject to the overriding authority of the earl, whereas the new Norman sheriffs acquired status as the lynch-pin of governmental administration, the main point of contact between the shire and the central administration. They took over the duties of the Old English sheriff in shire and hundred court and in the collection of the *geld* and they held down the local population. Those to whom they had once taken second place now held titles without power. The families of several Norman sheriffs attained the rank of earl within two generations; De Mandeville, Bigot, Durand of Gloucester and Edward of Salisbury are examples of this.

In the early years of the Conquest, before 1072, only three earls were created, out of William's local command-ers; Robert de Commines in Northumbria (but not for Yorkshire) in 1069, and two earls in Mercia, Hugh for Chester and Montgomery for Shrewsbury. William fitzOsbern, Earl of Hereford, was a special case as William's chief ally. Later in the reign the new earldoms tended to be confined to one shire, so eventually there was an Earl of Warwick, Henry de Beaumont, or an Earl of Kent, Odo of Bayeux; even though they might have been granted exten-sive powers, as Odo had been given in southern England or William fitzOsbern, Earl of Hereford, north of the Thames, their earldoms were still based on a shire rather than a province. The rank of earl thus became more of a personal honour or mark of royal favour, given to a man because he was powerful rather than to endow him with power. The earldoms of Chester or Shrewsbury were more equivalent to the counts found in France, because they were governing marcher territories where they needed to have a free hand, whereas others, holding in less threatened counties, ranked below them. The term *Dux* indicates the more important men. What distinguished an earl from a baron is not always clear. Earls may have led the military contingents from their shires or even held some of the king's demesne land, but the only certain privileges were an entitlement to the 'Earl's Third Penny' from the profits of justice in the shire courts, over which they presided along with the bishop.

Normans replaced Englishmen quite rapidly, not merely by 'natural wastage' as Englishmen aged and died, but also as a result of forfeiture arising from rebellion or exile. Some English sheriffs, like Marleswein of Lincoln, went into exile and from there plotted rebellion and the earls rebelled and ended up in prison or dead. Yet, if William was endeavouring to rule like an Anglo-Saxon king and as the Confessor's heir, why should the English have rebelled? They were, for a start, in a better position than we are to judge how much William's fair words were worth. Not all of his promises were kept. Even his own Normans were not entirely loyal, starting with Eustace of Boulogne. Others refused to stay in England and returned to Normandy or elsewhere, to the greater freedom of action available to them on the Continent. Few non-Normans remained at all, mainly Bretons, and some of those were to be driven into rebellion. Lower down the social scale the process of expropriation began with the forfeiture of lands belonging to all those who fought and died at Hastings. As the Penitential of the Papal Legate Ermenfrid reveals, this meant that all those who fought against William were treated as rebels. Ermenfrid's principal purpose was to impose penances for sins committed by Normans who had taken part in the invasion of England. It was issued by the Norman bishops and enforced by Ermenfrid, Bishop of Sitten, the Legate or representative of Pope Alexander. To kill or wound, even in battle, was a sin for which

penance had to be done to win remission of the punishment which might be suffered in Purgatory after death. The
Penitential prescribes a lesser penalty of one year's penance
for those members of the Norman army who killed men
in battle, as at Hastings, or in fighting those who resisted
William before his coronation, than for the killing of men
in other circumstances, as for instance during plundering
or ravaging, for which three years was imposed, but it also
prescribes the lesser penance for those who killed rebels
after the coronation. The Legate clearly equates men who
fought for Harold with those who engaged in rebellion.
In this way, the expropriation was justified and William's
claim to the throne recognised.

DISTRIBUTION OF THE SPOILS

From about January 1067, as the *Peterborough Chronicle* says,
William 'Gave away every man's land' at his Christmas
Court. Englishmen who wanted to retain their lands had
to make an appropriate payment to the king. Under the
year 1066 the same source insists that they had to buy
their lands. Those who had died in battle, or who had
already chosen exile or had been outlawed were unable
to redeem their lands in this way and the lands were confiscated and used to reward the king's followers. A good
example of what might happen is the case of Abbot Brand
of Peterborough, successor in late 1066 to Abbot Leofric
who had returned from the Battle of Hastings and then
died, presumably of his wounds. Brand, their provost,
elected unanimously by the monks, at first sought recognition of his election from Edgar the Aetheling, who was
very pleased to give it. As a Lincolnshire man Brand had
turned to the Aetheling because all the people of his part of
the world, the Fens, expected Edgar to become king. Even
Archbishop Ealdred of York and the Londoners had at first
supported the Aetheling because 'it was his proper due by

birth', and had been ready to proclaim him king. Perhaps word of this had reached the Fens, although there is no evidence that Edgar was ever consecrated king or that it was ever contemplated. This need not in itself have been necessary, English kings commonly ruled for months without being crowned.

William was furious and, in order to appease the angry king and after the intercession of a number of prominent men (one of whom might have been Ulf Topeson who witnesses a charter at this time), Brand paid forty marks in gold, a huge sum for the time, and received recognition of his appointment and confirmation of the abbey's title to its estates. (The gold mark was equal to £6, the pound to 20 shillings and the silver mark, which was equal to 13s 4d, existed only for accounting purposes. The only money in circulation was the silver penny, of which twelve made a shilling.) William probably also felt that to make an example of such a major abbot at that moment would be politically unwise. He was still trying to win over the English without the need for further bloodshed.

Similarly, Abbot Baldwin of Bury St Edmunds held Stoneham, Suffolk 'from the time when the English redeemed their lands' and paid two gold marks. He also paid £5 for another estate at Ixworth Thorpe. It was mainly Wessex and East Anglia which were affected by the expropriations at the commencement of the reign because they were occupied during 1067. Thus Abbot Aethelwig of Evesham obtained thirty-six estates 'by paying the appropriate price', according to Hemming's Cartulary. Elsewhere, lesser thegns paid smaller prices varying in amount from two gold marks to as much as £10. Another example has a monk of St Benet at Holme in Norfolk pay half a mark in gold to the king's reeve to discharge the forfeiture of the land of a free man and so got it for his abbey *absque licentia regis*, without licence from the king. An interesting case was that of Eadric, a freeman holding one carucate of land in

Saxlingham under Stigand, with sake and soke and 'after the king came to England, that same Eadric mortgaged it for one mark of gold and for £7, in order to redeem himself from capture by Waleran (the Crossbowman).' This process could work both ways. A certain Osbern the Fisherman had half a hide in Sharnbrook which King Edward's *huscarl* Tovi had held, and with it claimed another one and a quarter virgates; 'but after King William came into England he refused to give the rent from this land and Ralph Taillebois gave the rent and took possession of the land itself in forfeiture and handed it over to a certain knight of his.' On the other hand, a certain Alric held one virgate in Southill under Walter the Fleming which Leofwine, a thegn of King Edward's, had held in pledge, 'but after King William came to England he who had pledged this land redeemed it, and Seiher (Walter's brother) took possession of it to the king's loss'.

The abbeys profited from lending money to those who could not afford to redeem their lands from their own resources and then, if the loan could not be repaid the abbots could foreclose on the mortgage and seize the land in lieu of repayment. Abbot Baldwin received confirmation from King William of his title to all of the abbey's lands 'whether redeemed from his neighbours with his own money or acquired by their own free and voluntary gifts'. Meanwhile, those Englishmen who succeeded in retaining their lands did so by speedy submission and that meant mainly members of the royal household, such as stewards and butlers (*discthegns* and *hraeglethegns* in Old English), sheriffs and stallers, that is men with 'seat and special duty in the king's hall'. On occasion, if a man could not readily redeem his land or offered too little to satisfy the avaricious king, William would accept a better offer from someone else. The *Peterborough Chronicle* in its obituary of King William, obviously written when the king was safely dead, tells us that:

> The king gave his land as dearly to rent as he might possibly do for the dearest; then came some other person and offered more than the other had before given, and the King let it to the man who offered him the more. Then came a third and offered a larger sum still; and the King let it to the possession of the man who offered him most of all; and he heeded nothing how very sinfully the reeves obtained it from the miserable men, nor how many unlawful acts they committed; but the more it was said about true laws, so much more lawlessly did they act.

William of Poitiers says that after the coronation William 'distributed liberally' what Harold had 'avariciously shut up in the Royal Treasury', that is, used it to pay off his mercenary troops and reward his supporters. He distributed part 'to those who had helped him in the battle'. But the larger part, and that the most valuable, he used for the benefit of Norman monasteries (see the lists of lands held by Norman abbeys and priories in Domesday Book). He added to this 'tribute', which rich men and cities everywhere offered to their new lord. He says that William set a limit to this collection of tribute but the *Chronicle* by contrast records a heavy levy of the *geld* or land tax which 'oppressed the wretched people' and talks of the robbery of English monasteries and adds that 'all that they overran they caused to be ravaged'. Harold's banners, a richly decorated and jewelled figure of a Fighting Man and the Wyvern of Wessex went abroad to the Papacy in return for the consecrated banner sent by the Pope to William. Most gifts went to Aquitaine, Burgundy, Auvergne and the Kingdom of France, and most of all to Normandy.

The exact method by which estates of fallen thegns were identified so that they could be given to chosen barons is unknown. There must have been records of estates and their possessors kept by royal officials, lists indicating *geld* liability, for example, kept at Winchester, but if so, none have survived. Documents such as the *Inquisitio Geldi* show that it was known which estates were liable for *geld* and how much had to be paid. Some documents such as the *Burghal Hidage* and the *County Hidage*, which are still available to us, show that it was known exactly how many hides a shire was rated for, including beneficial reductions given to favoured landowners. Few other documents have survived, made redundant by the making of Domesday Book. It is likely that the oral testimony of shire and hundred court was also used. Once it was known that a particular thegn had large estates it would be a straightforward matter for the royal representatives, usually the Sheriffs or perhaps special commissioners such as were used in later enquiries, to require the shire court to identify the thegn's holdings. No doubt those bishops, stallers and others who were willing to collaborate gave evidence also. Domesday Book contains several references to this process, usually where it comments that the due process had not been followed. So William Malet is described as holding Holderness and the jurors say they 'saw him having and holding them (the lands)' but they have not seen the king's writ or seal for this. At Northorpe in Yorkshire, Ralph de Neville held land of Abbot Turold 'but did not have a livery officer for it'. A last example comes from Wallington Hundred, Sussex, where Walter de Douai 'had two hides of the king, as he says, but the men of the hundred say they "have never seen the writ or the king's commissioners who had given him seisin (possession) of it"'. The process seems clear enough and made good use of the English administrative invention, the writ.

The writ, as distinct from the diploma or charter, was an informal letter written in English and authenticated by an impression of the king's seal hanging from one corner. Its use seems to have originated in the reign of Aethelred and became common under Cnut. Writs were produced by the king's writing office, the staff of which passed as a whole into King William's service. The earliest writs of his reign are identical in style to those of King Edward but gradually it became common to issue them in Latin and to draft them along French rather than English lines.

The changes began with the appointment as Chancellor of Herfast, the king's chaplain, in about 1068, but were made very gradually and writs could still be issued in English even in 1085. The writ has been used in English administration ever since the eleventh century, mainly in the Law Courts, and was always known as a writ until comparatively recently when some denizen of the Circumlocution Office decided to abolish the name. The very use of the word 'writ' demonstrates that written documents were already essential to English government before the Normans came. The process of distribution of estates was not recorded in writing, it was left to the members of Hundred and Wapentake to remember what had been done. That is why they were questioned by the Domesday Commissioners to ascertain the facts of ownership. Grants made by the king would have identified the new lord and named his 'antecessor', as the previous landowner was termed. At the time of making the grant the king would specify the military or other service due from the grantee. He did this either by sending a writ, probably addressed to the sheriff, or by sending a livery officer who would grant 'seisin', feudal possession, to the new Norman landowner.

This wholesale expropriation of land was undoubtedly resented by the heirs and kin of the deceased or exiled thegns. These men or women would have expected to inherit estates. Even in the case of loan-land rented from the abbeys, on a typical lease for three lives, continuation or renewal of the lease would have been expected, but only niggardly amounts of land were left for the widows and orphans. Thus resentment bred a spirit of dogged resistance though many men preferred surrender to starvation.

The offence was compounded when the new Norman lords sought to marry the heiresses, widows and daughters of the deceased thegns. Those who willingly married a Norman were consorting with the enemy, but not all of these marriages were freely entered into. Lanfranc, Archbishop of Canterbury, in his *Letters* records that women in fear of a forced marriage entered convents and became nuns. One objection to this on the part of would-be suitors was that the land might pass to the abbey. Hemming, in his Worcester Cartulary, complains of the Normans 'usurping the inheritances of Englishmen', and this usurpation was also perpetrated by collaborators like Ralph the Gael and Abbot Aethelwig. All bishoprics and abbacies south of the Humber are found holding their lands by rendering military, that is, knight service, to the king. This burden was imposed on them either at the moment of submission or somewhat later, as when a new bishop or abbot had to be appointed by reason of death or deposition of his predecessor. The weight of this burden is revealed by the size of the *servitium debitum* as the number of required knights was termed.

The Bishoprics

Canterbury	sixty Knights
Winchester	sixty Knights
Worcester	sixty Knights
Lincoln	forty Knights
Salisbury	thirty-two Knights
Bath	twenty Knights
London	twenty Knights
Exeter	fifteen Knights
Chester	fifteen Knights
Hereford	fifteen Knights
Durham	ten Knights
Chichester	two Knights

York	seven Knights (but later twenty; heavily wasted in 1069)

The Abbeys

Peterborough	sixty Knights
Glastonbury	forty Knights
Bury St Edmunds	forty Knights
Abingdon	thirty Knights
New Minster	twenty Knights
Tavistock	fifteen Knights
Westminster	fifteen Knights
St Augustine's	fifteen Knights
Coventry	ten Knights
Shaftesbury	ten Knights

There were fourteen others with anything from six down to one.

After the siege of 1071 Ely had a punitive level of sixty knights imposed, later reduced to forty. William Rufus had demanded the full sixty but was persuaded to accept forty by Abbot Simeon, who was told to garrison the isle with forty knights. William I guaranteed to the abbeys the title to their demesne lands in order that they might be better able to render him military service. He especially ratified recent grants of land, made since King Edward's death, in order to increase their resources for supporting their knights. These at first were billeted on the abbey premises, even dining with the monks, and only later, when this was found to disrupt the life of the monastery, were fiefs created for them. This was the case also with bishops like Wulfstan of Worcester who were expected to contribute to the defence of the realm. He used the resources of his see to defend it against the incursions of the Welsh and the attacks of rebels, behaving in this respect like a marcher lord (as had bishops of Hereford before the Conquest). He even kept his force of knights as part of his episcopal household. They dined in his hall and lived within the bishop's house.

The Sees of the bishops and the abbeys made an important, even vital, contribution to the defence of the realm and to Norman control. In East Anglia, for example, the major abbeys, Bury, Ely and Peterborough, kept watch on the Fens and guarded the East Coast against the Danes. In Berkshire the abbey of Abingdon controlled the district north of the Thames as well as the Thames river crossing and the intersection of at least two major roads. It is this strategic importance of Sees and abbeys that, in part, explains the large garrisons of knights billeted upon them and their high quotas of military service.

In contrast, because of the lack of contemporary records, we do not have the original burdens imposed on the major barons, but they can be estimated from the returns of their successors in 1166 in answer to Henry II's inquiry, the returns to which are called the *Cartae Baronum* and record the knights enfeoffed under several categories. The most important is the number enfeoffed under the 'Old Enfeoffment' at the time of the death of Henry I. These are taken, in J.H. Round's explanation in his essay, 'The Introduction of Knight Service into England', to be the number originally imposed by King William, and range for the greater men from seventy-five for the great feudal holding called the Honor of Totnes down to fifteen barons with a quota of ten knights each. English magnates, lay and ecclesiastical, had often kept armed retainers in their households, known as *cnihts*, from which the word 'knight' is derived, and travelled about with them for protection. It was the resemblance between the English lord passing by escorted by his *cnihts*, and the Norman baron with his escort of *milites* or *equites* that led to the adoption of the word '*cniht*' for the new Norman horse-soldiers, the knights.

Huge areas of the country came under the control of the barons, especially those who as castellans or sheriffs commanded large bodies of knights. Such were Hugh d'Avranches, Earl of Chester, or Roger of Montgomery, Earl of Shrewsbury, or in Hampshire and the Isle of Wight, the rich and powerful Hugh de Port. In the North a huge fief was created for Count Alan of Brittany, who received the Honor of Richmond, so vast it became known as Richmondshire, and Holderness was held by a Fleming, Drogo de la Beuvrière. These examples illustrate the formation of the baronial fiefdoms known as 'Honors'. The overall impact of all this, combined with forfeitures resulting from the failure of rebellions, was to eliminate Englishmen almost entirely from the front rank of Anglo-Norman society.

3

Ruthless Imposition of Norman Rule

The year of the northern rebellion, 1069, was to be the turning point in William's policy with regard to English officials and servants. Use made of them came to an abrupt end. This was not because policy changed after the rebellions, although what that policy was now became clear, but because William no longer needed English officials as the collaborators had trained their Norman successors in running the administrative machine. Until then William can be said to have genuinely operated something like an Anglo-Norman administration.

Like France in 1940, the country was divided before 1069 into an occupied and an unoccupied zone and English earls still represented the king in the two-thirds of England still unoccupied. Earl Edwin in Staffordshire and Earl Morcar in Yorkshire, as writs show, retained some of the authority belonging to their rank. Earl Waltheof had been confirmed in office and Tostig's former deputy Copsige was sent to govern the North, while Cospatrick still represented the House of Bamburgh. So William still had five Englishmen as earls in the early years of his reign. But did anyone replace Earls Harold, Gyrth and Leofwine? Gyrth's earldom had been truncated and what was left, Norfolk and Suffolk, went to Ralph the Staller and from him to his son. Ralph, of course, was half Breton. Leofwine had been replaced almost exactly by Odo of Bayeux, who held all of Leofwine's earldom except for Middlesex. Even so, Robert fitzWymarc had authority over Essex. Lastly, Wessex; here, William fitzOsbern was in command, though without the title of Earl of Wessex. William is styled 'earl' on the king's return from Normandy in 1067, but without a territorial addition. He was not yet 'of Hereford'. His base was Winchester in Wessex and he certainly administered most of what had been Harold's earldom. But none of these men reaches the status of the great Anglo-Saxon earldoms which closely resembled dukedoms.

But 1069 was decisive. The north of England was taught the lesson that the South had learnt at Hastings. After the rebellion the balance of power inclined fully to the Norman side, as one might suspect it was always going to do, and no amount of lip-service to the forms of Old English administration could disguise the essential truth that William ruled through an army of occupation. Royal, and indeed baronial, castles had been spreading steadily northwards and by 1071 extended in a web of power and control from Exeter to Norwich, from Dover to Chester, and on to York. From Hereford to Norwich there stretched a military command in the hands of William fitzOsbern and Odo of Bayeux as Earl of Kent. William's characteristic method of control was to move by way of castle, walled town and monastery, all of which were defensible. A town might be simultaneously an earl's seat, a bishopric, an abbey, and a castle might be built within its walls.

Gradually, from 1067 onwards, it had dawned on the English lords just how insignificant they were in the Norman scheme of things and in the sight of the rapacious foreigners upon whose support William really relied, and this led inevitably to revolt. The defeat of rebellion was followed by an extension of the process of expropriation which had begun immediately after Hastings as the estates of the English were confiscated and distributed among the Norman magnates who were establishing themselves, as both warriors and landlords, and, by marriage, assimilating the remnants of that ancient landowning aristocracy. There then began the further distribution of the spoils of conquest as the magnates themselves parcelled out their lands in fiefs (estates or manors held by knight service) which they granted to their men and this completed the transformation of English society. It has been well observed that the clash and intermingling of races destroyed the ancient simplicity of English social relationships. The distinction between free and unfree rural population reappeared and exercise of royal authority was conditioned by the possession of property. Men sent to represent the king in the countryside or whose personal attendance upon him was no longer required were rewarded with land. William's very success brought him new landed property by which he could win over new retainers and establish royal power. That explains why so many landless knights had flocked to his banner. It was in this period that Abbot Aethelhelm of Abingdon, like other lords, gave manors to men who would hold them from his church and 'in each case declared what would be the obligations involved in its tenure'. For this he used the estates which had previously been 'held by men called thegns who had been killed in the Battle of Hastings'. One effect of this process was that the Church was in danger of losing control over its landed property to the new fief-holders or to powerful and rapacious neighbours.

Rebellion was followed by forfeitures which opened up the Danelaw, England north and east of the line of Watling Street, with Yorkshire and northern Mercia, to Norman occupation. England was now an occupied country held down by military force. Nowhere is this more clearly shown than in the widespread construction of castles. One estimate has suggested that there were as many as 400 by the year 1100. That would include many temporary and short-lived structures and not all of them would fit the usual picture of a Norman castle. The number of major castles was about eighty by the end of the reign and in the early period down to 1076 there were about forty. There were over twenty county towns with at least one castle. York had two and London three. Other substantial boroughs and towns with a castle numbered about ten. As the *Chronicle* for 1087 put it 'He had castles built and poor men hard oppressed'.

Orderic Vitalis is very clear about their usefulness. He points out that;

> The fortifications which the French call castles were very
> rare in the English regions and hence, although the English
> were warlike and bold, they were weaker in resisting their
> enemies.

The vast majority were of the type known as 'motte and bailey'. They were quick and easy to build and very effective. It is even said that at least one was brought over with the invading army in prefabricated form so that it could immediately be erected. These fortifications had arisen in northern France and the Rhineland in the early eleventh century. There lords had sought out 'high hills fortified by nature in uninhabited places and built castles there'. First the motte or mound was piled up by digging a large

ditch and using the spoil from it to form an artificial hill
or to enlarge an existing one. The tower or donjon was
erected on the summit and reached by means of ladders
which could be pulled up to make access more difficult.
All this used the forced labour of the local peasants. The
ditch around it might be filled with water from a stream
or spring. After that a large, open, relatively flat area was
created around the front of the motte and marked by the
building of a ring-work, consisting of an embankment and
ditch surmounted by a palisade. The local population was
required to do the manual work and in effect the ancient
obligation of *burh-bot*, work on the defences of the *burhs*,
became castle-work. Entrance to the 'bailey' was by way of
a defended gate and guard house. Other necessary living
and storage buildings, including stables, were built within
the bailey and this space was used as a training and exercise
area. The tower was not a residence but a lookout post
and a place of refuge in the event of the bailey falling to
the enemy. It dominated the surrounding countryside, a
symbol of Norman dominance. In the course of time these
castles were converted from wood to stone and became
more and more elaborate but the original motte and bailey
was effective enough for its time.

Armies on the move need defensible encampments and
from the beginning the Normans made use of existing
English and Danish encampments, former Roman fortifications and Iron Age forts, many of which are better
described as ring-works than as castles. At Dover the Roman
remains were part of the Saxon *burh* or fortified enclosure
(which occupied one part of the Roman structure) and
was regarded by the Normans as a castle even before the
Conquest. William put a motte and bailey castle inside the
existing walls. This was undoubtedly also done in other
burhs where a Norman castle is found in one corner of an
existing English burh, and such multi-occupation and use
provides some nice problems for archaeologists. It is worth

realizing that the word *castellum*, translated as castle, refers not to the motte but to the bailey, and *castellaria* are the enclosures around the mounds which bear the towers or donjons. This distinction is useful in any consideration of references to castles used or attacked by the Normans on campaign.

Not all Old English *burhs* or boroughs had defensive enclosures, some were enclosed but not fortified. One distinction between a *burh* and a castle was that whereas a *burh* occupied a median area of about twenty-five acres, or some 380,000 square yards, castles needed only a couple of acres, around 360 square yards. It was the advent of the Norman castle which often gave a defensible fortification to a *burh*. Some castles occupied sites away from the *burhs*, on which thegnly residences had once stood. These usually had a hall and, if surrounded by a fence or wall, a *burh* gate. Little evidence has survived of these halls as they were usually of wood and often now lie beneath stone or brick castles or manor houses. They are therefore difficult to find. At Sulgrave in Northamptonshire for example there is a ring-work which is believed to occupy the site of a thegn's residence, but the ring-work is post-Conquest and does not coincide with the Saxon enclosure. Sulgrave was later said to have had a castle which must refer to the ring-work, that is a site defended by bank, ditch and palisade, as the Saxons did not build castles. To consider London, for example, the town itself was walled and there were fortified houses within them, as the one called Paul's *Burh* shows. It stood within the cathedral precincts. William started the building of the White Tower and there were two other castles later known as Montfichet and Baynard's Castle (after Henry I's sheriff William Baignard). The only castles mentioned in England before the Conquest were built by the Norman relations and allies of King Edward. The *Chronicle*, under 1052, mentions the 'castle' in Herefordshire built by the foreigners, that is Earl Ralph of Mantes, King Edward's nephew, and his Norman followers.

The Normans attributed part of their success in overcoming the English to the lack of castles. Their view was that had the English had such defences they could have held out more successfully. Yet in previous centuries the *burhs* had saved England from the Danes. According to the Burghal Hidage, men were required to man the walls of a *burh* with four men to every five and a half yards (a pole), or 160 per furlong. These fortified enclosures, often surrounding a town, had repelled the Danes and provided strong points for resistance, but by 1066 the system seems to have been allowed to decline after twenty years of relative peace under King Edward. A few places still had impressive defences, Wareham in Dorset (converted to a castle by King William), Wallingford in Berkshire and Cricklade in Wiltshire. Only lack of will to resist fostered by collaborators can explain why these places did not oppose the Normans. If other *burhs* had required William to lay siege to them, as Exeter did, the strength of the Norman army might well have been eroded and spread too thinly to hold down the country.

A COMPARISON

It might be useful here to compare William's approach with the treatment meted out to the English by Cnut the Great, after his defeat of Aethelred II and Edmund Ironside. Cnut governed firmly, restoring the peace, order and security desired by his subjects and refraining from antagonising the English. Indeed, he deliberately set himself to conciliate them. He confirmed the great families in their positions of authority at the time of the creation of the earldoms, especially Mercia and Wessex. His accession was not followed by a systematic forfeiture of estates or oppression of the peasantry. His was the last in a series of Danish invasions which had created the Danelaw, which included Northumbria, the Five Boroughs (Lincoln, Nottingham,

Derby, Leicester and Stamford), East Anglia and the
south-east Midlands, occupied by a largely Anglo-Danish
population. The contrast with William is quite marked.

In 1018 Cnut declared his intention to enforce the laws
of his English predecessors and proclaimed in 1020 that
he would govern with the advice of the bishops. He then
issued Law Codes based on the enactments of the earlier
kings. There is no evidence of any code of laws issued
by King William. The laws attributed to him by twelfth-
century lawyers are their own compilations based on the
texts available to them of codes issued before the Conquest,
with a few additions known to have been made by the
Conqueror. He claimed to rule as common lord of the
whole country united by language and literature. But this
became true of the Norman kings only in the twelfth
century. The English and Danes shared a common culture
as the epics *Beowulf* and the *Song of Maldon* show. Even
Edward the Confessor as king was fond of telling old Norse
tales to his courtiers. Cnut had brought Englishmen and
Danes into a common political society. But the Normans
and English did not begin to share language and literature
until the thirteenth century at the earliest.

Cnut appointed Englishmen to the most important
of his earldoms (which now replaced the Old English
Ealdormanries) and the one action of Cnut which had the
most influence on events after his death was his division of
the country into a number of earldoms. Over a dozen different earls are mentioned in his charters, but he appointed
Englishmen in the southern earldoms; Wessex went to
Godwin, Mercia at first to Eadric Streona the former
ealdorman and then to Leofric who was a member
of an old Mercian family. Bernicia was left to the
care of the House of Bamburgh supervised by the
Danish Earl Siward who held Northumbria. Elsewhere
there were Scandinavians, in East Anglia, Yorkshire,
Worcestershire and Herefordshire. This was done because

such delegation of royal authority could not be avoided if his rule was to be effective. William, on the other hand, appointed major Norman magnates like Odo his half-brother and William fitzOsbern, his steward, to rule the southern half of England and, after the death and rebellion of Copsige and Cospatrick, he sent a Fleming, Robert de Commines, to rule Bernicia, with disastrous results.

It had been expected that William would do as the Danish kings had done and confirm existing families in their positions of authority, especially when new earls were created to replace the Godwinson clan. But this did not happen. The earldoms of the Godwinsons disappeared completely. Exceptionally, Earl Edwin of Mercia remained fully in office but his brother, Morcar, who retained his title, was not sent to carry the king's rule into Northumbria. Even Earl Waltheof, who retained his Midlands earldom, had little authority to go with it. Other men discovered that they could retain their lands, but only at a high price. The leading men of the Canterbury lands and of London retained their property and, if loyal, their fathers' rights, but under Norman lordship. The lands of those who had gone into exile went the same way as the lands of those who had fallen at Hastings or in other battles. These lands were distributed to William's followers.

After the initial submissions King William had continued his progress through southern England and by the end of 1066 all prominent men in the South, including the Aetheling, had submitted because the faction in favour of it had prevailed. The duke then secured the formality of his election to the throne by the Witan, and accepted English laws and institutions as far as they were useful to him in securing the obedience of the English. But they were more and more interpreted in favour of the Normans, especially the land laws. Yet he is complimented by Orderic, basing himself on the lost ending of the *Chronicle of William of Poitiers*, for passing 'many wise, just and merciful provisions whilst he was still in London. He ordained certain laws and established them firmly'. These are the amendments to the Law of King Edward mentioned in later codes of law drawn up in the twelfth century.

Leaders of Anglo-Saxon opinion such as Ealdred, Wulfstan and Aethelwig headed a native group determined to support William. He had made them believe that he wanted a genuine Anglo-Norman state although this was never a real possibility because of the need to reward his followers, so dispossessing the deluded English. It might be the case that at first the collaborators encouraged William in his seizure of the estates of the Godwinsons in the hope that this would satisfy his demands. In fact it was nowhere near enough. The Norman land-grab spread and the new landowners, during the first stages of the occupation, were accompanied by soldiers, and messengers of the king were sent into the shires armed with writs to distribute the estates.

The support of the collaborators could not disguise a ruthless policy of terrorisation, the mutilation of hostages as at Exeter in 1067 and the devastation of arable land between Hastings and Canterbury. William was later to spend a year 'wasting' the north of England in 1069 and 1,000 square miles became a wilderness with no inhabited place between York and Durham. Even Cheshire, Staffordshire and Derbyshire record ten per cent of their estates as 'waste' in Domesday Book. In truth, the Conquest was a brutal and violent takeover resulting in the deaths of thousands.

The Old English earldoms began to disappear after the rebellion of 1068. In that year, as will be seen, the king took personal command everywhere, only appointing local commanders when necessary, and only three of those are termed 'earl', that is, de Commines in Northumbria (but not Yorkshire), and Mercia divided between Hugh at Chester and Roger of Montgomery at Shrewsbury. Earl

Roger had a *praesidium regis* at Shrewsbury, usually signi-
fying a castle and the presence there of a *comes* or count.
William may have intended to retain some earls in the
English tradition, which would explain why Roger styles
himself *Dux* (the usual Latin for 'earl') and why Chester
was given such wide powers. But if he did, the concept
was swept away in the aftermath of the rebellions. The
king limited the number of earldoms, creating only four
before 1071, out of military necessity, and of these Hereford
and Kent had ceased to exist before the end of the reign.
The others, Chester and Shrewsbury, remained 'palatine',
that is outside the normal royal administration, and were
joined by Durham after the rebellions. Other new earls
were less prominent in government than the English earls
had been. Those earls, like Odo and fitzOsbern, who were
so prominent did not derive their influence or power from
their title of earl but from a direct commission from the
king. William I preferred instead to run local government,
except on the Marches, through sheriffs who did not, as in
the Old English system, have an earl over them, and the
shire became a *comitatus* or county, though governed by a
vicecomes called a sheriff, and not by a count or earl.

If William had ever intended to rule in the English
tradition, success would have depended on the extent
to which he could rely on English loyalty rather than
Norman military power. He might, at first, have tried not to
antagonise those Englishmen who accepted him, confis-
cating only the lands of the Godwin clan, and of dead or
exiled thegns, with which to reward his followers, yet still
by 1087 there were only three major southern English
landowners. The reason is not difficult to discern. The
English did not continue to acquiesce in William's rule,
especially when what they regarded as their legitimate
aspirations were ignored. They were in constant negotia-
tion with the Danes, as William of Poitiers testifies, and
there was that 'sullen spirit of rebellion'. So the risings

began in 1067, peaked in 1069 and did not wholly die away until the 1080s. Great stretches of the countryside were ravaged in consequence and refugees streamed out of Yorkshire into Scotland (where they contributed to the Englishing of the Lowlands) and down into the Midlands, besieging Abbot Aethelwig of Evesham, seeking his aid.

Exiles and misfits ended up on the shores of Ireland, Flanders and Denmark, and for that matter, Scotland. Those who had taken refuge in Ireland, using Dublin as a base, as the sons of Harold and their followers had done in 1066, continued to make raids into the deep inlets of Devon and Cornwall, stirring up risings. This caused concern to both William I and his son William Rufus, who had to take measures to guard their shores against invasion from Ireland. That is why they encouraged settlement on the northern shores of the Bristol Channel and down into Devon and Cornwall. As late as 1098 Gruffydd ap Cynan and Cadwgan ap Bleddyn recruited Irish-Norse auxiliaries for use in North Wales in alliance with Magnus Barefoot of Norway who arrived with a small fleet. William of Malmesbury believed he intended an invasion and was accompanied by Harold son of Harold Godwinson. They were repulsed although Hugh of Montgomery was killed in the skirmish.

The Normans at Hereford, backed by their bishop, Walter, had their own role, to create a bridgehead into Wales using the survivors of Edward the Confessor's 'French Connection', fitzScrob, fitzRichard (of Richard's Castle), and Alfred of Marlborough. Eventually William fitzOsbern was sent to the borders as a trouble-shooter after the revolt of Eadric the Wild. He almost certainly received lands there previously held by King Edward and probably those of Morcar, Harold and Queen Edith as well. To secure the area, fitzOsbern built castles at Wigmore, Clifford and Chepstow and re-fortified Ewias Harold. He was in fact exercising the authority, holding the lands and almost the rank, of Earl Harold, with most of his responsibilities, 'farming' the shire like an earl and sheriff combined. But, as already stated, he is never styled 'Earl of Wessex'.

It is no surprise that the sons of Harold and their men went to Ireland, and eventually to Flanders, since Earl Godwin of Wessex and his family sought refuge in both places during the crisis of 1051 when Godwin quarrelled with the Confessor. Harold himself and his brother Leofwine went to Ireland and the rest of the family went with Earl Godwin to Flanders. Earl Tostig, during his exile, married Judith, the daughter of Count Baldwin. After 1072 the Aetheling and his followers also took up residence for a time in Flanders until the wreck of Edgar's fleet caused him to seek the aid of his brother-in-law Malcolm, King of Scots. Maerleswein the Sheriff of Lincolnshire and Cospatrick son of Maldred, Earl of Bamburgh, and their men were also exiles in Scotland. Denmark is known to have received exiles who were welcomed at King Swein's court, notably Eadric the Steersman of the Abbey of St Benet at Holme, Norfolk, and Ringulf of Oby, a man of the abbey, joined his lord, Abbot Aelfwold, there. The abbot and his men had been charged with defence of the east coast in 1066. Another who preferred exile in Denmark was Aethelsige, prior of St Augustine's Canterbury and administrator of Ramsey Abbey.

There is convincing evidence from the *Chronicle of Abingdon Abbey* that the situation in the early years of the Conquest was a volatile one. Abbot Aethelhelm is said to have:

> deemed it necessary never to go about without an armed retinue, for, in the midst of the conspiracies which broke out almost daily against the king, he felt compelled to take measures for his own protection.

So castles were built at Wallingford, Windsor, Oxford and elsewhere 'for the safety of the realm' and the abbey was ordered to provide guards for the castle at Windsor. Aethelhelm then employed an armed force of knights, that is, mercenaries, for this purpose. Only later 'after the disturbances had died down' was it then 'noted in the annals' how many knights were to be demanded from the bishoprics and abbeys for the defence of the realm. These 'emergency' conditions described in the *Chronicle* are also illustrated by the laws introduced or enforced to control the behaviour of the English. They were introduced by the Norman king because he was obliged to take measures to secure the safety of Norman settlers. We do not know precisely when these laws were enacted but they could well date from this early period as Orderic's testimony indicates.

THE MURDRUM FINE

So many Normans were turning up dead in suspicious circumstances 'in this strange land, in lonely places' as one text puts it, that William I introduced the *murdrum* fine payable if the victim was a Norman. Any hundred in which a Norman was found dead was expected to hand over the man responsible, within five days according to one source, but if he escaped and they could not produce him in court, then the fine was levied. The earliest reference gives a fine of forty-six marks, forty to the king and six to the relatives. This was collected for all unsolved murders of free men, though usually at a much lower rate. From *murdrum* we derive our term 'murder' for premeditated killing and the distinction between that and 'manslaughter'.

One way to avoid having to pay was to show that the victim was an Englishman, and this became 'Presentment of Englishry', whereby the victim was identified by his kin to show that he was not a Norman. The *Dialogue of the*

Exchequer from Henry II's reign maintains that the English secretly ambushed Normans and slew them, which looks like the action of the *silvatici* or wildmen. The *Dialogue* comments that William I 'subjugated and distrusted' the English and that after putting down their rebellions he sought out all those who had fought in the war against him, and their heirs, and deprived them of all hope of recovering their estates.

In addition to the *murdrum* procedure, we are told that the Normans took up and made more effective the pre-Conquest system of tithings. This was a system put on a regular footing by Cnut in his Secular Code. All free men over the age of twelve years were required to join a group of ten men, a tithing, led by a tithing man, if they wanted to be able to defend themselves against a charge of wrong-doing. Each of the members was required to guarantee the good conduct of his fellow members and sometimes a whole village might go to make up a tithing. They were obliged to produce in court any member of the tithing who was suspected of a crime and to raise the 'hue and cry' and pursue him if he fled. Failure to hand over the suspect or to catch him resulted in a fine.

This pledge of good behaviour derived from the Old English idea of *bohr* or security and the Normans fused this with the tithing system to create 'frankpledge'. The sheriff was required to see to it that all tithings had their full complement of members and that every man obliged to join a tithing was actually in one. These tithings were smaller, more manageable and personal bodies than the Hundreds, which were also obliged to arrest and pursue suspects, and so they were more effective in maintaining social control and producing suspects in court.

These two procedures, tithing and *murdrum*, are mentioned in the lawbooks produced in Henry I's reign by lawyers seeking to establish what the law was in an easily accessible form. They are pseudepigraphic, taking the form of law codes allegedly issued by William I (and Henry I). The *Ten Articles of William I* makes it clear that all free men who wished to retain their free status had to join a frankpledge 'so that the frankpledge may bring him to justice' should he offend. The *Leges Willelmi* in Cap. 22 imposes the fine of forty-six marks and in Cap. 25 imposes the frankpledge system. The *Ten Articles*, Clause 2, reveals that William I required all free men to swear allegiance to him, so making a traitor of anyone who opposed him and Clause 3.1 seeks to protect 'all the men whom I brought with me', by imposing a fine for failure to arrest a murderer within five days.

The former English ruling elite realised, after the rebellions had been put down, that England was going to be entirely Normanised. King William's policy of making use of Englishmen in the upper levels of his government alongside Norman lords had failed. What is not clear is the extent to which there had been an honest attempt to include Englishmen in government. It can be maintained that William had hoped to maintain a policy of inclusiveness. It is argued that use was made of the English officials of the household (despite the fact that he replaced Regenbald as head of his secretariat by appointing Herfast as chancellor in 1068), that English sheriffs were retained, even that he kept the surviving earls in his entourage and made no attempt to remove them from their earldoms. In the Church he also retained both English archbishops (even if allowing that Stigand was bound to be replaced sometime) and removed no English bishop or abbot before 1070.

Against this is the evidence for his whittling away at the authority of the remaining earls. He installed Norman earls along the Welsh border in Mercian territory, he gave 'authority and jurisdiction' over seven Mercian shires to Abbot Aethelwig of Evesham, and he failed to keep his promise to Earl Edwin of marriage to one of his daughters.

He ignored Morcar altogether, appointing a succession of Norman nominees, Copsige, Cospatrick and then Robert de Commines to govern Northumbria.

It is possible to argue that the rebellions destroyed the original policy and that William only gave up his intention of governing with a combination of Normans and Englishmen after the English had repeatedly rebelled. But it can also be argued that his policy fuelled resistance and that he had always intended that it should. Resistance provided the excuse needed to justify further expropriation of lands and offices. This is to argue that the king provoked the rebellion of 1069, by the appointment of Robert de Commines, having come to the conclusion that no matter whom he sent, the Northumbrians would never willingly submit, and that he did so at a time when his castles had been given sufficient time to accumulate supplies and men (significantly only the castles at York were taken by the rebels, in peculiar circumstances) and it was logistically possible to bring a large army into the region.

The reality probably involves both arguments. This is to say that William at first attempted to make use of the English elite because he needed them to allow him to establish his rule effectively and that had they remained co-operative he might have continued to do so. But from the beginning it became clear that not all of the English were prepared to submit indefinitely, especially when they found that the rewards of co-operation were rare. In addition, William needed to reward his followers and the expropriations which followed Hastings were insufficient to satisfy demand so that it became necessary to find a way to justify further confiscations. That justification was provided by the rebellion of 1069.

4

Repression, Revolt and Rebellion

The essential political point made by William's coronation was that he was the legitimate heir of Edward the Confessor, to whom he was related by blood. The Confessor's mother, Emma, a daughter of Richard I of Normandy, was William's great-aunt, and thus he was, in the Norman view, a member of the English royal family. As such he had been accepted by the Witan led by Archbishops Stigand and Ealdred, the Earls Edwin and Morcar, and the greatly respected Wulfstan, Bishop of Worcester. Above all, God had favoured him by granting him victory on the field of Hastings.

To avoid conflict between the occupying forces and the population suitable rules of conduct were laid down. Public order was to be maintained and the use of violence of any sort was forbidden. Orderic Vitalis says that 'He forbade disorders, murder and plunder' (Margery Chibnall's rendering of '*seditiones, caedem et rapinam*') – more bluntly, insurrections, killing and robbery. Thus, he says, 'restraining the people by arms and the arms by laws.' But as the legitimate heir of the Confessor, William now took the view that his reign had begun with the Confessor's death and, therefore, to have taken up arms against him was treason. Those who had fought, and died, at Hastings were to be treated as rebels and their estates forfeit to the king who could dispose of them as he wished. This is made explicit in the writ sent to Abbot Baldwin of Bury St Edmunds commanding him to surrender the lands of those 'who belonged to St Edmund's soke and who stood against me in battle and are dead'.

The estates of the Godwinsons were confiscated and added to the royal demesne which now extended into every shire and amounted to over 14,000 manors. This meant an income in rents of some £11,000, about double that of King Edward. In addition, a very heavy levy of the *geld*, the land tax, was imposed, which 'oppressed the poor people'. A *geld* was usually raised at a rate of two shillings on the hide which was capable of producing 72,000lbs of silver. In practice, little effort was made to distinguish between the lands of those who had died at Hastings and those who had died at Stamford Bridge or Fulford. Nor did the Normans make any distinction between those lands a thegn held which were his own inalienable property, held *in propria libertate*, and other lands held on lease, as it might be for three lives, or an annual rental, as tenant of an abbey. For example, a rich thegn called Turchil had done homage to Abingdon Abbey and Abbot Ordric, for land at Kingston. When he died at Hastings the Norman Baron Henry de Ferrières seized his land for himself despite the abbot's protests and the fact that the lordship over the land had been vested in the abbey long before the battle. This baron also took the land of Godric, Sheriff of Berkshire, after he died at Hastings, including land at Fyfield, held on a lease of three lives in such a way that the abbey was to suffer no loss no matter what might befall the tenant. Yet Norman writers, such as Orderic, say that those who submitted were 'allowed to keep all their possessions honourably when they had sworn fealty' although he also tells us that William toured the kingdom, appointing castellans to their castles, and 'distributed rich fiefs that induced men to endure toil and danger to defend them'. It was then that the 'fortress' at Winchester was given to William fitzOsbern, 'his vicar over the whole of southern England'. Odo was given 'Dover and the whole county of Kent' and he left them in charge, assisted by Hugh of Grandmesnil, Hugh de Montfort, William of Warenne and a number of others.

WHILE THE CAT'S AWAY THE MICE DO PLAY

So by March 1067 William felt secure enough to return to Normandy, which was now demanding his attention because of the effects of his prolonged absence in England. He was to remain there for most of 1067. With him went his 'honoured guests', those members of the Witan who had collaborated in the establishment of his rule over the occupied area of the country and whose co-operation had guaranteed the acceptance of Norman rule in their bishoprics and earldoms.

Thus a number of these '*Prominente*' went to Normandy, more as hostages perhaps than as allies. With the king were, Edgar the Aetheling, the Earls Edwin, Morcar and Waltheof, Archbishop Stigand and Aethelnoth, Abbot of Glastonbury. None of these were fully trusted. William of Poitiers indeed explicitly remarks that he took with him those whose loyalty he particularly suspected so that during his absence no revolt instigated by them might break out and the general populace, deprived of their leaders, would be less capable of rebellion. He says that William thought it essential as a precaution to hold in his power as hostages men whose authority and safety were of the greatest importance to their kinsmen and compatriots. Being subjected in this way they carried out his orders most compliantly, for even if he chose to express a wish they interpreted it as a command.

SHADES OF 'WORKING TOWARDS THE FÜHRER'!

Stigand's claim to be archbishop was canonically suspect by reason of charges of simony and pluralism and because he had accepted an archbishop's pallium from an anti-pope. William had decided to allow the Pope to decide his fate 'because of the very great authority he (Stigand) exercised over the English'. The lands of the three earls had not yet seen a Norman soldier, nor had Gloucestershire.

In William's absence the situation in England rapidly deteriorated. No matter what fair words William might have uttered about respecting the laws of King Edward and the rights of the English, those he left in charge saw things in a different light. The Conqueror's half-brother, Odo, Bishop of Bayeux, was now ruling Kent and left to govern the occupied area south of the Thames as far west as Hampshire, while William fitzOsbern, Steward of Normandy, and now earl, was given charge over the whole area north of the Thames from his earldom of Hereford in the west to Norwich in the east and as far north as the borders of Mercia on the Humber and the Trent.

Now whether it was that these two had weaker control over the activities of their men than had been exercised by the king or whether they simply did not care, those of their men who were guilty of rape and pillage not only went unpunished but were actually protected by their lords. The two earls proceeded to hold down the areas committed to their rule by force. Castles were built to enforce control. As the *Anglo-Saxon Chronicle* put it; they 'built castles far and wide throughout the country and distressed the wretched folk', and the Chroniclers accuse them of over-weening pride and of ignoring the protests of the English, rendering them no justice. Orderic insists that 'some of these men governed their people well; others irresponsibly heaped heavy burdens on them'. Domesday Book records that in 1086 Ralph de Tosny held a castle at Clifford built by fitzOsbern on the land of a thegn called Bruning. William fitzOsbern's men in the castle of Hereford were particularly oppressive, seeking to force thegns on the Welsh borders to come in and make their submission to the king. Of course, William of Poitiers, whose account of William's rule is noted for its tone of propaganda, paints a different, more favourable picture. He praises the moderation in government of the two earls, but he was writing before 1080 and for the court while others, like Orderic Vitalis, wrote when the earls were safely dead and could not resent what was written about them. Orderic's picture is a grim one.

But meanwhile the English were groaning under the *Norman Yoke*, and suffering oppressions from the proud lords who ignored the king's injunctions. The petty lords who were guarding the castles oppressed all the native inhabitants of high and low degree and heaped shameful burdens on them. He adds that fitzOsbern and Odo,

> swollen with pride, would not deign to hear the reasonable plea of the English or give them impartial judgement. When their men-at-arms were guilty of plunder or rape, they protected them by force, and wreaked their wrath all the more violently upon those who complained of the cruel wrongs they suffered.

One might almost be in Occupied France under the Nazis reading a report of the activities of Gauleiters. Later Orderic was to claim that the Normans became over-wealthy on the spoils garnered by others and arrogantly abused their authority. He says that they 'mercilessly slaughtered the native people like the scourge of God'.

In September 1067 a sideshow developed in Kent, notable only for hesitant English participation in it which makes it a harbinger of what might yet come. Eustace of Boulogne, husband of King Edward's sister Goda, had been promised rights of some kind over Dover by his brother-in-law. After the Conquest, he felt slighted because William had ignored his contribution at Hastings and made no effort to endorse his rights at Dover. He, therefore, responded to an appeal by the Kentishmen for aid. Goaded to rebellion, they sent ambassadors to Boulogne urging Eustace to equip a fleet with soldiers and arms and hasten to the attack of Dover. Although he had previously (especially in 1051) been seen as their bitterest enemy, they now, knowing of the jealousy that existed between Eustace and William, and 'of his experience, his prowess in war and fortune in battle' made their peace with him. Expecting his protection, their idea was to hand over to him the fortress at Dover to hold against the king. His attempt was a dismal failure. He acted as they had requested and hurried across, hoping to catch the castlemen by surprise. He had many knights, but few horses, but 'all the neighbouring countryside was armed'. The custodians, Odo of Bayeux and Hugh de Montfort, were away, as was the greater part of the garrison, a favourable opportunity for a determined attacker. Had the assault lasted longer many more Englishmen would have joined the attack, but the garrison rallied and resisted staunchly, even making a sally against Eustace's force. He hesitated and retreated. This was fatal. The garrison cut his rearguard to pieces and the rest, thinking Odo had arrived, panicked, some perishing down a precipice. Many died. The knights charged and slew all that they could and Useless Eustace leaped on his horse and escaped ignominiously by ship, probably in high dudgeon, back to his county of Boulogne, while his English allies carefully dispersed.

TROUBLE ON THE WELSH BORDER

A much greater problem was developing in Herefordshire. On the surface it seems unconnected with what was going on elsewhere, but this is deceptive. As the fundamental cause of unrest was everywhere the same, it gave rise to similar reactions. Orderic complains that a large number of the English were plotting rebellion because of their desire to recover the liberty they had once enjoyed and had now lost, but that many, keeping faith with God, revered the king.

The castlemen of Hereford had for some time been harassing a local thegn by the name of Eadric because he had refused to make his submission to King William. He was one of the richest pre-Conquest thegns in Shropshire and cousin to Siward the son of Aethelgar (who had married a daughter of the famous Eadric Streona, Ealdorman of Mercia in Cnut's reign). He was said by Florence of Worcester to be the nephew of the ealdorman but that writer is a generation out and it might be that his father Aelfric was the nephew rather than the brother of Eadric Streona. Nonetheless, Eadric was a member of the family of an ealdorman of Mercia. He is also probably the Eadric of Wenlock who held land as a tenant of Much Wenlock Priory in 1086.

In summer 1067 Eadric, with the assistance of the Welsh princes Bleddyn, King of Gwynedd, and Rhiwallon his brother, King of Powys, attacked the castle of Hereford, which had just recently been completed, laying waste Herefordshire as far as the River Lugg before returning to his own lands. Thus Eadric was the first to adopt guerrilla tactics. It may be that his attack was intended to focus Norman attention on the Welsh borders while others prepared their own attacks elsewhere. The Norman mailed knights could not cope with the lightly armed mounted men of the Welsh hills, just as later in the Fens they had problems with Hereward's men moving around in boats. Norman heavy cavalry was quite unsuited for use in mountainous areas or in bogs and was better on broad rolling plains. This did, for a time, restrict the invaders whose techniques of warfare were not always superior to those of the English. Orderic Vitalis, confusingly, seems to think that Eadric then made his submission to King William, but as his chronology and geography are both confused in this section of his Ecclesiastical History, he has put this too early in Eadric's career.

For some time after that the garrison seems to have left Eadric alone and he remained at large on his estates in Herefordshire and Shropshire until some time in 1069. It was in that year, according to Orderic, that the leaders of the English Resistance sent messages over all England to raise support and there was a general outcry against injustice and tyranny. Men were asked to bind themselves by weighty oaths against the Normans (which has a parallel in 1070 at Ely where Hereward and his men bound themselves together by oaths over the tomb of St Etheldreda). This suggests that the Resistance was in fact both more widespread and better co-ordinated than appears from the scattered accounts of revolts given in the *Anglo-Saxon Chronicle*. Other sources insist that there were rebels hiding out in woods and marshes where they planned their risings and which they used as bases from which to attack any Normans they encountered. Thus was born the guerrilla movement of the *silvatici* (woodsmen, foresters or wildmen) as these men were known to the Normans. These are the fighting men described by Orderic Vitalis when writing about the nature of the English Resistance. He says that some men chose to live in tents, despising those who lived in houses as too soft and flabby and says that from this custom of theirs they were called *silvatici*. It may be that their 'tents' were like the 'benders' used by those who in the present day occupy woods lying in the path of road-building schemes, that is made of branches covered with cloth or hides and so well camouflaged. These 'wild-men' no doubt dressed in garments which would act as camouflage in the woods and marshes, just as outlaws in later centuries were reputed to wear 'Lincoln Green'. It is possible that stonemasons responsible for the decoration of churches saw fit to include memorials to these men and that country people, in creating outdoor shows and plays, wrote in a part for these 'wildmen of the woods'. Carvings and paintings of the figure called the 'Green Man' are found in many churches. There are at least eight in Norfolk alone. As the *Oxford English Dictionary* has it, a 'Green Man' was someone dressed in greenery to represent a wild man of the woods and took part in rural shows. They are described as 'woodmen or wildmen, green men covered with green boughs'. St Peter and Paul, Salle, Norfolk has a painting of a bearded man's face peering through green branches and leaves. There is nothing demonic or pagan about it. That at least some of these figures are covert memorials erected to the memory of local *silvatici* is a real possibility, even if in later centuries they became a conventional motif used by carvers and painters.

The Resistance in France in the 1940s were known as the *maquis* because they hid in the scrub and bush, and to *prendre le maquis* was to 'go underground' and become a partisan. To be *silvaticus* was to hide in the woods or other wild country, away from the Normans, and to lie in wait to ambush them. The cognate Latin verb, *silvescere*, means to run wild and *homines silvestries* are woodsmen. The English equivalent of *silvaticus* was 'wild'. In some entries in Domesday Book concerning Eadric, the clerk has interlined beside his name the word 'salvage', that is 'sauvage' as a Norman French version of 'wild', and at least two other men have the nickname 'Wild'. William of Poitiers agrees that there was a general conspiracy, although he gives no date for it. That the Earls Edwin and Morcar were the leaders of this Resistance movement cannot be directly demonstrated, but those promoting it certainly sought their support, and they themselves are reported to have 'wandered at large in woods and fields'. The *Abingdon Chronicle* says there were many plots and claims that men hid 'in the woods and some in islands, plundering and attacking those who came their way. Others called in the Danes and men of differing ranks took part'.

The *Chronicle of Evesham* also, after reporting William's ravaging of the North, naming Yorkshire, Cheshire, Shropshire, Staffordshire and Derbyshire, claims that this was done on account of 'the outlaws (exules) and robbers who hid in woods and damaged many people'. However, Orderic is, as usual, well informed. He says that the English 'groaned aloud for their lost liberty' and plotted cease-lessly to find some way of 'shaking off the yoke that was so intolerable and unaccustomed'. Some are reported to have sent messages to Swein of Denmark, urging him to claim the throne, won by the sword of his ancestors, while others fled into voluntary exile hoping to find in their banishment freedom from the power of the Normans or to secure foreign aid to come back and 'wage a war of vengeance'.

The year 1068 saw a rebellion, somewhat tentative in practice, by Edwin and Morcar in conjunction with their Welsh allies. They engaged in what Orderic terms 'a fierce insurrection'. He tells us that the cause was William's fail-ure to keep his word. After Edwin had made peace with the king, William had given him authority over his brother and one third of England (that is, his own earldom plus that of Morcar) and promised him the hand of one of his daughters in marriage but the king then listened to 'dishonest counsels' from 'envious and greedy followers' and broke his word. Edwin's patience had thus run out. This first rising soon collapsed but after this, so William of Malmesbury says, the Earls Edwin and Morcar 'disturbed the woods with secret robberies' rather than meet the king in open conflict. This fits in well with the picture which can be drawn of the career of men like Eadric and the Exile Hereward. It is one of small-scale guerrilla warfare by partisans like the *maquis* in France during the Second World War. What can be pieced together about Eadric the Wild confirms this interpretation.

While the Conqueror was fully engaged during 1069 with the rebellion in the North, the Welsh border went up in flames. Again Eadric, aided by the surviving Welsh prince, Bleddyn, and the men of Chester, seized the opportunity to revolt. It may be that Eadric was disturbed by the promotion of Roger of Montgomery to be Earl of Shrewsbury and his building of the castle there. This time Eadric attacked and seized the town of Shrewsbury but was unable to take the castle. This is a clear indication of the vital role played by these strong points in maintaining Norman rule.

Leaving the castle untaken in their rear, and so by-passing the Norman garrison, the rebels moved on to Stafford and were again resisted by the castlemen there. Further attacks were launched in Cheshire and to the east of Stafford. Unable to capture the castles anywhere, the rebels had to be content with ravaging the countryside and its Norman settlers. The local commanders found themselves confined to their castles, unable to act together to overcome the revolt. This suggests that this was a more successful tactic than first appears because William was forced to leave Yorkshire and intervene in person. He advanced on Stafford and there, according to Orderic, annihilated the rebel force in an easy victory. Again an English army had no effective answer to the Norman cavalry and might well have been outnumbered. There is no indication that anyone again attempted to meet William in open combat. From there William moved to Nottingham, intending to return to York, drawn back by reports of a renewed effort by the Danes to occupy the city.

At York he found the Danes gone and the northern rebels dispersed once more into the 'woods and marshes', returning to their guerrilla tactics. This withdrawal and dispersal suggests that some English commanders favoured 'Fabian' tactics in which an attack in force is made and as much damage done as possible, followed by a rapid retreat when the enemy threatens an overwhelming counter-attack. William's reaction was to order an intensive search to be made in order to root them out. Then, having launched this campaign, and after establishing that the rebel leaders had returned to Scotland, he returned via York and across the Pennines to Cheshire where peace was not yet fully established. At Chester he found, as so often elsewhere, that his mere approach had been enough to end the troubles. It was surely then that the thegn Eadric made his submission, early in 1070.

The role of the *silvatici* is clear. In between periods of open rebellion they carried on a war of attrition against the Normans, the kind of action that was to cause William to introduce the *murdrum* fine. Then, when any kind of organised rebellion began, these men would leave their hideouts and join in the fighting, fading away again if things went wrong. It is possible that the identity of some of these men, in addition to Eadric, is known; that is, Wulfric Wild who had land at Newton in the South Riding of Lincolnshire and Wulfwig Wild who held land in Atterton, Shelving and Perry in Kent. There was also a messuage in Dover held by Ranulph de Colombières 'which belonged to a certain exile, that is outlaw' and this could be Wulfwig. Others are identified as outlaws, men like Skalpi, a thegn of Harold's, who went away to York 'in outlawry' and died there, or Aelfric, a freeman of Stigand's, who was outlawed and

Eadric, King Edward's steersman who 'became an outlaw in Denmark' and even Thurstin of Thetford, a freeman commended to St Benet of Holme, 'and he was an outlaw because Aethelwig (the collaborator) of Thetford made him an outlaw'. What the *silvatici* could not do, without outside help, was drive the Normans out. For this, like the Resistance in Europe during the Second World War, they needed an army of liberation. For the English in the eleventh century, the only possible source of such help was Denmark, and the Danes, having no intention of fighting a pitched battle with William, let them down.

ALARUMS AND EXCURSIONS IN THE SOUTH WEST

The situation which had brought William back from Normandy on 6 December 1067 had resulted from the oppressive behaviour of the Earls of Kent and Hereford. He had, says Orderic, heard evil reports which 'hinted that the Normans were to be massacred by the hostile English', supported by the Danes and other barbarous peoples. One reaction to their oppression came from the town of Exeter. This was a spontaneous decision by leading burgesses to defy the Normans, possibly fomented by the presence of Gytha, mother of Harold Godwinson. Her flight suggests that she had played some part in the Resistance. That the citizens, or some of them, were the prime movers is certain. They had prepared for their act of defiance all through 1067, strengthening the walls and towers, recruiting allies in other south-western towns and raising levies of extra soldiers.

In December they threw down the gauntlet, refusing to swear fealty to William as other towns further east, like London and Winchester, had done. They would render to him the same dues as they had paid to King Edward but they insisted on maintaining their ancient rights and, when he arrived, refused to allow him to enter the town.

Their protest was certainly against the increase in the *geld* and against attempts to increase other customary dues paid by townsmen. It was also a refusal to accept the status of vassals.

After celebrating Christmas in London, when he was 'gracious to English bishops and lay lords' and 'at great pains to appease everyone', the king willingly granted them favours which, Orderic acidly remarks 'often brings back to the fold persons whose loyalty is doubtful'. After that, every city and district which he had visited in person or occupied with his garrisons, obeyed his will. He warned his Normans 'never to relax for a moment' as men in the borders were still barbarous and had only obeyed even King Edward 'when it suited their ends'. Then Exeter became the first town to be dealt with. William's reaction was to march on the town and lay siege to it. Warfare in northern France and Normandy rested in part on a series of sieges and the Normans were particularly well versed in the art of siege warfare using siege towers and ballistae, or catapults. Over-hasty assaults were launched by the Normans, seeking to impress their king, and these resulted in heavy casualties. The Norman troops also suffered from the weather in a harsher-than-usual winter. But all was not well within the town. A peace party inevitably developed in the ranks of the thegns who owned property in the town and who feared the loss by forfeiture of their lands outside. They sought to sue for peace and gave hostages but the more hawkish citizens persisted in their defiance and refused to surrender even when William blinded one hostage and hanged another in sight of the walls. But in the end the peace party prevailed, and after a siege of eighteen days, opened the gates to the king. Gytha and other 'wives of good men' made their escape and fled to Steep Holm in the Bristol Channel. William was magnanimous in victory, to show the benefits of collaboration. Those who had surrendered were treated moderately, just as prominent rebels

during the next few years were received back into favour
if they submitted. This state of affairs was to come to an
abrupt end after the siege of Ely.

From Exeter, therefore, he required only submission and
payment of the customary dues. Their ancient rights were
recognised. In particular these included the right to pay
geld only when London, York and Winchester paid it, and
then it was a half mark of silver 'for the use of the thegns'.
Exeter also served on military expeditions in the same way
as a vill of five hides (like Barnstaple, Lydford and Totnes),
which would mean providing one fully trained and armed
soldier. But, of course, they had to accept the building of
a castle, Rougemont, and Domesday records the result:
forty-eight houses were destroyed, 'since the king came
to England', to provide space for it. The Norman garrison
was placed under the command of Baldwin de Meules,
Sheriff of Devon, brother to Richard fitzGilbert, Lord of
Tonbridge and Clare. They were the sons of Count Gilbert
of Brionne who had been one of William's guardians.
Baldwin was also given charge for the time being over
the whole Cornish peninsula which had, as yet, seen no
Normans. The fall of Exeter was swiftly followed by the
submission of the other towns of the South West and particularly by the submission of Gloucester and Bristol.

William had now taken effective measures to secure
control of the region, as the fate of later English risings in
the South West shows. The Exeter rising, with its attempts
to involve other towns, and the participation of Gytha
and her supporters, might have been intended as part
of a more general uprising. Certainly it was followed, in
summer 1068, by the arrival of the sons of Harold, that is
Godwin, Magnus and Edmund, with a fleet provided by
Diarmaid of Dublin. They raided the Bristol Avon, landing
at Avonmouth, but were driven off by the Bristol men and
'could gain nothing from the borough'. They then went
into Somerset where they were confronted and defeated by

the shire levies commanded by Eadnoth the Staller, Sheriff of Somerset. Many men were killed in the battles, on both sides, notably the Staller himself, but the Godwinsons were forced to retreat to their ships and return to Ireland.

These attacks by the sons of Harold threatened for a while to become annual affairs but they returned in the summer of 1069 for the last time. Sailing as before from Ireland with sixty-four ships, possibly some 3,000 men, they arrived at the mouth of the Tavy in Devon. But this raid, like the others, received little support. On this occasion they were opposed by the new Breton lord of Cornwall, Count Brian, 'with no little army', and by William Gualdi, and were driven off. There were apparently two 'battles' in one day, for which read skirmishes, the usual form of warfare in the eleventh century. They returned to Dublin and, says Orderic, Ireland was 'filled with mourning', and from there, finally, went to Flanders to join Gytha in fruitless exile. Thus they were to play no part in the risings which accompanied the arrival of the Danes. Evidence of the effects of this raid comes from a document, made for the Bishop of Exeter, known as the 'Exon Domesday' which records that nine manors in Stanborough Hundred were still waste in 1086 because they were 'wasted by the Irish'.

Those risings in the West Country and incursions by the sons of Harold were left by the king to be dealt with by local commanders, just as he largely left the Welsh border and Cheshire to those in command there. It was the same after the news of the arrival of the Danes sparked off a series of local risings in the South West after the departure of Harold's sons. As well as the risings beyond Selwood and in western Mercia, there were rebellions in Devon, Cornwall, Dorset and Somerset. Exeter was attacked but remained loyal and then Robert of Mortain's castle of Montacute was besieged. The siege was raised by Geoffrey of Coutances with men from London, Winchester and

Salisbury while Exeter's citizens repelled the attack on the city, leaving the attackers to the tender mercies of the Norman relief column under Count Brian and William fitzOsbern. The assistance given by the English themselves in putting down these risings must be noted. No doubt men like Aethelwig, Abbot of Evesham and Edward of Salisbury helped to provide English levies when these were needed. As Orderic reports, 'At that time Ealdred, Archbishop of York and some of the other bishops were 'acting in the king's interests' and 'some of the most able citizens of towns and some native knights (i.e. thegns) of wealth and good name, rose unequivocally on the Norman side against their own fellow countrymen'. The bishops were of particular importance because of the location of their sees. Ealdred had responsibility on the southern marches against the Welsh: Stigand's see commanded an arc facing the Continent from The Wash to the Isle of Wight, with Sandwich as his manor. There was a military motive behind William's approval of the decision of Remigius of Dorchester to move his see to Lincoln which, like Durham, commanded the road to the North.

Aethelwig was one of the few abbots to earn William's complete trust and that explains his judicial responsibilities in seven shires, Shropshire, Herefordshire, Worcestershire, Staffordshire, Warwickshire, Oxfordshire and Gloucestershire. This made him little less than what was later termed a justiciar, with both judicial and executive powers. He was an important agent in keeping the peace and enforcing order, all the more so after the death of William fitzOsbern but probably while he still lived, also. An early writ of the Conqueror addressed to the abbot requires him to organise the assembly of the feudal host due from the barons of his province.

Several monasteries had military significance because of their position. Glastonbury dominated the Somerset marshes, just as Peterborough and Ely kept guard over the Fens. Tavistock commanded a deep inlet of the Tamar. This explains the military burdens placed on them, as on the bishoprics, and the replacement of English abbots with more reliable Normans, beginning with the appointment of Turold to Peterborough. After these flurries of activity, the rest of the South West remained quiet. Central southern England, under men like Aethelwig and Wulfstan, had accepted Norman rule. There is no sign of rebellion from shires south of the Thames. Those who had prospered under the Conqueror, like Edward 'the Rich' of Salisbury, Sheriff of Wiltshire, and Thurkill of Arden and other thegns and sheriffs, preferred to support the New Order in England.

THE NORTH IN REVOLT

The Northumbrians had taken no part in the battle at Hastings and in the immediate aftermath of the Conquest kept largely to themselves. The Sheriff of Lincolnshire, Maerleswein, a nobleman from the Danelaw, had probably undertaken the administration of the province after Morcar's defeat at Fulford and was at first left alone by William for whom the question of the North had no priority. The king was led to believe that Copsige, the former deputy to Tostig, was best fitted to obtain the taxes he wanted from Northumbria, and so in February 1067 Copsige was sent as earl to York. William had presumed this man, as a former creature of Tostig's, would be pliant and able to use his local influence. The Northumbrians had as yet seen nothing of the Norman army and thought little of these 'Frenchmen'. They had seen Macbeth's French soldiers easily beaten by Earl Siward and would have known how little Earl Ralph's Frenchmen had achieved in Herefordshire. As for Copsige, he proved as unpopular as Tostig. He too had the disadvantage that he was neither a member of the Bernician House of Bamburgh nor of the

family of Earl Siward the Dane. Shortly after his arrival in
the North he was set upon at a banquet and beheaded by
Earl Oswulf, son of Eadwulf of Bamburgh, and a protégé
of Morcar just as Copsige had been Tostig's man. Oswulf
and his partisans had fired a church in which Copsige
took refuge and caught him as he escaped the flames. This
was not so much an anti-Norman gesture as the rejection
of rule by a southern government. The purchase of the
earldom from William by Cospatrick, Oswulf's cousin, in
the December of 1067 was an attempt to prevent William
sending another southern appointee to rule the North.
William had not created a new earl simply because for
most of 1067 he was absent in Normandy.

Cospatrick proved no more able to raise taxes for the
king than Copsige. William's demands were far higher than
those of King Edward, who for part of his reign at least
appears not to have collected any *geld* at all, and were fiercely
opposed by the Northumbrians, whose determination to
resist had perhaps been made all the firmer by Archbishop
Ealdred's efforts to persuade them to submit. Cospatrick in
any case concluded that to 'farm' the taxes would not be
profitable (a 'farmer' of taxes paid them to the king himself
and then exacted as much extra tax as he could from the
unfortunate people) and made little effort to take up his
duties. Instead he went to Scotland where he joined up
with the Aetheling, Edgar. This prince had for some time
realised that the rapport between himself and the new king
was declining and he no doubt felt himself slighted. There
had been no open breach but the Aetheling had not been
offered a post in William's regime of the sort his rank might
have led him to expect. Early in 1068, therefore, he had
taken his mother and sisters with him and sought refuge at
the court of King Malcolm of Scotland. There he had been
joined by Maerleswein, and now by Cospatrick.

William was still far too busy to worry about the activities of these notables. He had recently dealt with the revolt

at Exeter and now turned his attention to impressing upon his newly conquered territories the full splendour of his royal status. He brought his wife, Matilda, to England and on 11 May she was crowned queen. As for the king, he now instituted the custom of a thrice-yearly crown-wearing, when the new king appeared before his court in full regalia as an anointed monarch, with crown, orb and sceptre. This ceremony was held 'three times a year, Christmas at Gloucester, Easter at Winchester and Whitsun at Westminster'. These were occasions of great state and the intention was to impress upon those present the full authority and majesty of William's kingship. Coronation had emphasised the religious nature of his office and these formal crown-wearings reinforced the message. It was at this point that William's hubris might have brought its attendant nemesis. He had assumed that it was now safe to bring the Duchess Matilda to England and make her queen. The coronation had been attended by many prominent Englishmen and yet it was to be followed by a series of rebellions through which the native aristocracy lost all that remained of its political influence.

5

The North in Flames

S hortly after Matilda's coronation William was made aware of discontent rising in Mercia and the North. As the *Worcester Chronicle* (D) for 1068 has it: 'Then the king was informed that the men of the North were gathered together and meant to make a stand against him if he came.' Resistance had begun to coalesce around Earl Edwin (who had absented himself from the queen's coronation) who no doubt felt threatened by the castle building going on along the Welsh border and might also have felt slighted by the authority given to Aethelwig of Evesham, which extended into three shires of Edwin's earldom. Earl Edwin had allied himself to Bleddyn of Gwynedd (Eadric the Wild's ally).

But the real bone of contention would have lain in the North, which had not yet formally submitted and showed no sign of doing so. Perhaps, too, the northern thegns had tried, like Exeter, to bargain with the king. William's response had been to set out on a military progress north, building castles as he advanced. The castle at Warwick (of which the motte or mound, known locally as 'Aethelfleda's Mound', still stands within the castle walls), was committed to Henry of Beaumont (later Earl of Warwick) which had the immediate effect of bringing Edwin and Morcar to renew their submission. The castle garrison and the royal army together had threatened the Mercian heartland and overawed the earls. Another castle went up at Nottingham and was left in the charge of William Peverel. Yet the threat from Mercia may well have been more serious than it now looks because Edwin and Morcar had not dared to give battle. Instead they and their men had proved unwilling 'to face the doubtful issue of a battle' and 'wisely' preferred peace to war and sought the king's pardon, which, to outward appearance, they secured. It is also the case that there is no real evidence to suggest that the Northumbrians acknowledged any right on the part of Morcar to command them.

Orderic relates that large numbers of leading men from England and Wales had met together because of the general outcry against Norman injustice and tyranny. He says that they sent messengers into every corner of 'Albion' (the whole island) to incite men either openly or in secret to act against the enemy, to get ready to act. Prayers were said in churches throughout the land for the success of the rising. It was in his account for this year that he provided his testimony about the *silvatici* and said that the rebels prepared to defend themselves in woods, marshes and creeks as well as in some cities. York, he says, showed no respect for its archbishop, Ealdred, and seethed with discontent.

Edgar the Aetheling had been accepted in the North partly because of Cospatrick's support, as well as that of King Malcolm and of the Danish nobleman, Maerleswein. Cospatrick's own participation seems to have been a matter of impulse. Just as it became necessary to act, the earl was distracted by news of Malcolm's men harrying in Bernicia in revenge for an attack by Cospatrick's men on Cumberland a few months earlier. The exact sequence of events is obscure but the effects are plain enough. Malcolm had intended to attack down the western side of the Pennines but had lost control of his wild Scots who began harrying Edenvale. The Yorkshiremen and Maerleswein were fortifying sites on the Humber and in the swamps and woods of the West Riding (sites to which they retreated when their leaders fled to Scotland). The idea had been to hold the Humber-Aire line while awaiting the assistance of the Mercians and their Welshmen and possibly the arrival of the Danes. Cospatrick was thus caught out by the speed of William's reaction. He turned back for Scotland where he not only made peace with King Malcolm but also accepted asylum there for himself and the Aetheling while negotiations (which proved fruitless) were opened with King William through Bishop Aethelwine of Durham, sent by William to seek an agreement. The rapidity of Cospatrick's retreat helps to explain the collapse of the opposition to King William in 1068, especially at York, where the citizens hastily submitted, along with those Yorkshire thegns who had not gone to Scotland or into hiding.

Reaching York, William entered the city unopposed. All signs of rebellion had faded away at his approach. Archill, the most powerful of the Northumbrian thegns, made peace and surrendered his son as a hostage. William built a castle there, on what is now Clifford's Mound, and left it in the charge of Richard fitzRichard with 500 knights as garrison. William Malet became Sheriff of Yorkshire. Returning south down the east coast, William built a chain of castles at Lincoln, Huntingdon and Cambridge, which must have gravely worried the Fenmen. The building of castles always had a punitive effect. Not only did a castle dominate the countryside around, providing a secure base for squadrons of knights, it also took up space within the town from which it took its name. This meant that every town lost many houses, pulled down to make space for the castle. At York matters were even worse. The Coppergate area was flooded and the River Foss dammed to make a moat. Despite this apparent success the Normans had failed to destroy their enemy's military strength and had not proved the English tactics unworkable so that this was only a partial success for William. The northerners had reacted in three ways: some submitted, some fled to Scotland, and the lesser men faded away into woods and marshes to become *silvatici* once more. Thus they adopted the classical guerrilla tactic: strike while the enemy is least expecting an attack and scatter into hiding when he reacts in force. The objective is to keep the enemy busy so that he cannot relax, wear down his resolution, weaken his man-power and resources, all the while awaiting the arrival of a relieving force large enough to take him on level terms. That is what was hoped for from the Danes, but, as events show, the Danes had other ideas.

Among those who returned to the king's favour at this time was Aethelwine, Bishop of Durham, who had been chosen as a mediator with Malcolm, King of Scotland, who listened to his embassy and accepted the terms offered, preferring peace to war with William still so close at hand. Malcolm sent the bishop back accompanied by ambassadors who swore fealty and obedience to William, or so Orderic asserts. The terms cannot have been to William's entire satisfaction. They can hardly have meant an acknowledgement of William as Malcolm's overlord for the Kingdom of Scotland. More likely, Malcolm saw himself as recognising William's rights over debatable areas like Cumberland. Certainly Bishop Aethelwine had done himself no lasting good in William's eyes.

William was now concerned to retain the services of the barons and knights who had come with him to England and renewed his offers of lands and revenues and promises of great authority, having, as Orderic says, 'completely rid the kingdom of all his enemies', or so he probably thought. The barons continued to be perturbed by the continual risings but feared to be branded as 'cowardly deserters' if they left England. Some did so nonetheless, claiming that their wives were missing them, and so forfeited the chance of English fiefs. Although few details are recorded by the Chroniclers, Orderic repeatedly insists that there had already been many tribulations inflicted on the rebellious English. He speaks of fire, rapine and daily slaughter wreaking destruction and disaster on the wretched people and complains that the land was utterly laid waste. This would have applied wherever the king and his army passed by just as in the early years of Henry I's reign a visitation from the royal court with its army of servants, courtiers and hangers-on meant economic disaster for the area in meeting their demands.

FIRE, SWORD AND SLAUGHTER

While the rebels awaited his next move, William decided that it was time to appoint a Norman governor for the far north, beyond the Tees, leaving Yorkshire to the Castellan of York and the sheriff William Malet. His choice fell on Robert de Commines who was made Earl of Bamburgh to replace Cospatrick. Leaving the castlemen at York to hold the shire, he went to Durham in December 1068 with an escort of 500 knights and occupied the bishop's house. He proved to be a man in the same mould as Odo and fitz-Osbern, arrogant and rapacious, and his actions ensured that the reaction of the northerners when it came would be savage. He treated his new province as in need of conquest, ravaging the countryside in the January of 1069. He treated the men of Durham 'as if they had been enemies', looting their homes and allowing his men to plunder unchecked. In effect, he paid the wages of his men by 'licensing their ravages and murders'. Bishop Aethelwine warned him to expect trouble and was ignored. The Norman should have known better. St Cuthbert's land was 'a whirling chaos surrounding the emerging power of Malcolm of Scotland'. It was eminently possible in these men's eyes that a Scandinavian kingdom might be re-established in the North or that a realm might be created for the Aetheling, Edgar, supported by the Danes and Malcolm, and crowned by the Archbishop of York.

The Northumbrians laid siege to the bishop's house when de Commines was known to be within and set fire to it when unable to take it by storm. The house burnt down and the earl and all his men perished by fire and sword. It is an event comparable to the assassination of the Governor of Bohemia and Moravia, Heydrich, in 1942, and led to inevitable reprisals.

The whole affair now escalated into a full-scale rebellion. Those who had taken Durham now moved towards York where they were to be joined by the Aetheling, Maerleswein and Earl Cospatrick and all their men. There is no evidence that this was pre-planned but we do know that the English leaders had been sending out messengers to rouse support among the citizens of York and in the rest of England. They also renewed their appeal to Swein of Denmark for assistance. William of Jumièges, in an undated passage, seems to be referring to events after the murder of Robert de Commines. He says that the northern thegns held a castle with a most powerful rampart, called Durham. From there, says the writer, they attacked the Normans while awaiting the arrival of King Swein of Denmark to whom they had sent messengers requesting his aid. They had also sent men to enlist the support of the people of York in their cause, furnished that city with men, arms and money and then 'chose as their king a certain boy, nobly descended from the stock of King Edward', that is, the Aetheling.

Certainly, as soon as it was known that Northumbria had risen, following the killing of Robert de Commines, Edgar and his supporters, with Cospatrick, raised their own fleet, expecting that seaborne raids might offer the best hope of defeating King William.

The leaders of the Northumbrians included not only the members of the ruling House of Bamburgh but also the descendants of Thorbrand the Hold, leader of the Danes of York. He gave his title to Holderness, much of which was his territory; the promontory of the *Hold*. (A *Hold* was a member of a class of Danish free men with a wergild or blood price twice that of an ordinary thegn.) Thorbrand had supported Cnut the Great and was therefore the opponent of Styr son of Ulf who supported King Aethelred. During these conflicts Thorbrand ambushed and killed Uhtred of Bamburgh who was on his way to make his peace with Cnut. Thorbrand's eldest son Carl or Karli, also a *Hold*, had in his turn supported Earl Siward of Northumbria.

These men were all connected to one another either by blood or marriage, and if not that, by feud. That Cospatrick son of Maldred and Arnkell son of Ecgfrith could appear in the same cause as the four sons of Karli Thorbrandson reveals the depth of Northumbrian anger. These ancient enemies sank their differences in opposition to the Normans, and the English now gained confidence from this success in resisting them. Orderic again tells us that they forgot fealty and oaths and the safety of hostages in their anger at the loss of their patrimonies and the deaths of kinsmen and fellow countrymen. The three forces which mattered most in the North now coalesced; the Northumbrians from between the Tweed and the Tyne, St Cuthbert's Men at Durham, covering the land between Tees and Tyne and the Yorkshiremen from the Tees to the Humber. Most of the planning was the work of the House of Bamburgh and the leading thegns of Yorkshire supported by Maerleswein, the former Sheriff of Lincolnshire who had been left by King Harold to govern the North after the defeat of Morcar at Stamford Bridge. It is probable that he should be regarded as Morcar's deputy, representing his views.

The citizens of York joined the rebellion because, like the men of the Welsh Marches, they resented the imposition of a castle within their city, and the behaviour of the garrison which inflicted every possible injury on the local population. The Norman settlement of Yorkshire had already begun. A writ dated to 1069 addresses 'all my thegns French and English in Yorkshire'. William Malet, Gilbert de Ghent and William de Percy had established themselves there by 1069. Gilbert had Hunmanby, an estate which had belonged to Karli, and William Malet had land in Holderness, (three estates belonging to Cnut the son of Karli) and de Percy held Whitby. The Domesday jurors were to claim that they had never seen either the king's writ or his seal for William Malet's holding. There were other complaints about this man seizing estates unjustly.

The rebel host now demanded that the citizens of York recognise the Aetheling as king, just as they had demanded that they recognise Morcar as earl in 1065. A major blow to his chances of coronation had been Archbishop Ealdred's decision to side with King William and so render himself unavailable to crown Edgar.

William himself never discounted the possibility of an Archbishop of York crowning a pretender. Hugh the Chantor, writing at York, commented on the manoeuvres which led to Thomas of Bayeux accepting his subordination to Lanfranc as senior archbishop saying:

It was expedient for the unity and solidarity of the kingdom that all Britain should be subject to one Primate; it might happen otherwise in the king's time or in that of one of his successors, that some one of the Danes, Norwegians or

Scots, who used to sail up to York in their attacks on the
realm, might be made king by the Archbishop of York and
the fickle and treacherous Yorkshiremen, and so the kingdom
be disturbed and divided.

After all, those fickle and treacherous Yorkshiremen were
still prepared to support a Danish invader even in the
months after the harrying of the North.

At York, in a rash move, Richard fitzRichard the
castellan made a sally from the castle and was caught by
the rebels. He and his men were massacred. William Malet
immediately shut himself up in the castle and sent for help.
William, who had made a short visit to Normandy, immediately returned on hearing news of the seizure of York
and, summoning his host, advanced on York in a series of
forced marches rivalling Harold's feat in 1066. Like Harold,
the Conqueror came upon the enemy outside the walls of
York, 'by surprise from the south with an overwhelming
army and routed them, and killed those who could not
escape, which was many hundreds of men'.

Thereafter he remained in York while a second castle
was built on Baille Hill, and made Gilbert de Ghent its
castellan. A punitive expedition northwards, by Flemings
led by Gilbert and sent against Durham, failed. According
to Simeon of Durham a black fog enveloped the king's
men, frustrating their attack. He attributed this to the
miraculous intervention of St Cuthbert, whose relics lay at
Durham. William now left his faithful lieutenant William
fitzOsbern to finish mopping up at York. The English are
said to have made one further attack on both castles which
was a failure as they were counter-attacked, possibly 'in
one of the baileys' or perhaps in the fosse or ditch outside, as Orderic claims, by William fitzOsbern himself. The
king returned to Winchester for Easter where he held his
crown-wearing as usual. But despite his success he now
took the precaution of sending Queen Matilda and his son

Robert to safety in Normandy. He had good reason. The rebel leadership was still at large. Most had escaped William by way of the Humber and gathered in Scotland where they received fresh recruits to their cause. One of the most important of these was Earl Waltheof who resented having been twice passed over for the earldom of Northumbria, and although he had been allowed to retain his earldom in the East Midlands, had seen the building of two royal castles within it, at Huntingdon and Cambridge.

Another significant figure was Siward Barn, a thegn with lands in many counties including Nottinghamshire, Derbyshire and Lincolnshire. He was a rich man with land in seven counties rated in total at over 100 hides. The heavy *geld* levied by the Conqueror was a burden he could well do without. He too would have been alarmed at the construction of royal castles in the East Midlands. That there may have been others is suggested by the list of those exiles found at the court of Swein of Denmark, like Eadric the Steersman and Aelfwold of St Benet's at Holme, men with East Anglian connections, drawn to the cause by Waltheof perhaps. When we recall the stories of his encounter with Gilbert de Ghent, it is not impossible to imagine that Hereward too may have joined the rebellion at this time.

THEN CAME THE DANES

What King Swein's motives really were is now unknown. Orderic Vitalis, as usual, has his own explanation. Swein, he says, was 'moved by the death and disaster which had overtaken his men in Harold's war'. As we know that William of Poitiers thought there was a Danish contingent at Hastings, it may be that the reference is to that, but if so, why did he wait until 1069? Perhaps, in some sense, he regarded the Anglo-Danes in the English army as his men. Certainly he is known to have made a claim to the English throne.

Orderic has a garbled version of the grounds for this claim, saying that Swein was nephew to King Edward and son of Harthacnut. In fact he was cousin to Harthacnut, as son of Cnut the Great's sister Estrith. Edward was half-brother to Harthacnut. Nonetheless, Adam of Bremen claims that Swein told him that he had been promised the succession by Edward himself.

Edward had been unwilling to decide on a definite heir, despite pressure from the Witan to make a decision, preferring, it seems, to leave the question in God's hands. Instead he seems to have played a diplomatic charade with each of the pretenders in turn, promising or hinting first to one man and then to another, like a rich uncle with several nephews who promises each in turn that 'one day all this will be yours'.

The arrival of the Danes in early September 1069 was not a bid for the throne. Such a move does not fit in with the Northumbrians' insistence on recognising Edgar as king. But if Danish motives are therefore obscure, their actions were plain enough. Swein was too cautious to come in person. He had no wish to repeat the fate of Harald Hardrada. He had received many messages from the English begging for his help and sending him subsidies to encourage intervention. Instead he sent his brother, Osbjorn, in command of a fleet of 240 ships accompanied by two of his plentiful supply of sons, Harold and Cnut, and Christian, Bishop of Aarhus. Orderic claims that other countries sent help also, notably Poland, Frisia, Saxony and even Lithuania. He says they sent 'many auxiliary troops'. Osbjorn followed the usual Viking pattern, testing the strength of the defences at Dover and attacking Sandwich, Ipswich (where the local defenders killed thirty Danes) and Norwich where Ralph of Gael repelled him. Osbjorn destroyed ships as he went but was repeatedly driven off by local levies. William was in consequence left with no useful fleet. During 1069 and into 1070 he fought the rebels with his land army. Not until Ely in 1071 did he make use again of butsecarles (sailors who could also fight) in surrounding the isle.

Between 15 August and 8 September the Danes arrived on the Humber and there met the Aetheling and his allies 'with all the Northumbrians and all the people riding and marching with an immense army, rejoicing exceedingly'. The only dissenting voice, that of Archbishop Ealdred, who might have been able to mediate, was silenced by his death on 11 September, worn out and distressed. William, who was hunting in the Forest of Dean, was warned of the advent of the Danes and sent orders to William Malet in York who replied that the castles could hold out for a year if need be. He was never more wrong. To prevent the rebels using them to fill up the ditches of the moat around the castles, the castlemen set fire to a belt of surrounding houses. The fire rapidly got out of control and consumed the entire city including the Minster. Two days later the combined forces of the English and the Danes made a ferocious assault on both castles and overwhelmed the garrisons. Only William Malet and Gilbert de Ghent and their immediate families survived and were taken prisoner. Earl Waltheof distinguished himself as he 'alone killed many of the Normans in the Battle of York, cutting off their heads one by one as they escaped through the gate'. No wonder, then, that his participation in the Revolt of the Earls in 1075 led to his own beheading.

This was to be the Normans' worst defeat in England. The intention of the rebels was now to seek revenge on the Normans and even to drive them out of the country. To exploit the success, Edgar sent messengers all over England to rouse resistance. The news did indeed spread and there were risings, as we have seen, all over the western part of the country, from Cheshire to Cornwall. Despite the success of the attack on the castles at York, the victory proved pyrrhic since it left the city a burnt-out wasteland. The rebels were unable to use the city as a stronghold from which to defy William and equally unable or unwilling to meet his mailed horsemen in the field. Despite that, they were able to hold him back at the Aire for three weeks.

GOVERNMENT BY PUNITIVE EXPEDITION

William did not make the mistake a lesser commander might have made. He left his local commanders in the affected areas to deal with their own problems and concentrated on preventing the Danes from penetrating south of the Humber, which might have altered the whole picture. At the news of his approach the Danes withdrew from devastated York, a smoking ruin which they might not have felt worth defending. Instead they tried to fortify the Isle of Axeholme, just as they were to make use of the Isle of Ely in 1070. The Aetheling's men, without Danish support, were easily dealt with by the garrison of Lincoln castle and the rest of the larger rebel force dispersed at the approach of the royal army. William, satisfied for the moment, left his lieutenants Robert of Mortain and Robert of Eu to keep watch on the Danes while he himself dealt with the rising in western Mercia.

Returning to Nottingham at news of a Danish intention to reoccupy York, he advanced by way of the Trent and the Aire, where removal of the only bridge delayed him for three weeks until a ford was found, enabling him to reach York. There he found that the Danes had once more retreated to their ships on the Humber and that the Earls of Eu and Mortain, having no ships, had been unable to pursue them. There on the Humber the Danes were being kept supplied by the men of the marshes, though the Normans took strong action to prevent this. William opened negotiations with Osbjorn. He allowed the Danes limited foraging for supplies and even promised to send them some himself. Osbjorn was simply offered bribes which were readily accepted and in return the Danes agreed to return to Denmark in the following spring, asking only to be allowed to stay for the winter on the Humber. This was acceptable to William as it left him free to deal with the rebels as he wished and left the North exposed to the full fury of the king as the rebel host took to the hills expecting William to rebuild his castles, which he did, and to return south, which he did not.

The Danes seem to have been paralysed by William's reputation for invincibility. Their problem was their lack of cavalry. Their traditional tactics depended upon fighting an infantry battle and they had no answer to the Norman knights. Perhaps the legend of Stamford Bridge was already in circulation with its tales of Englishmen on horseback cutting down Hardrada's men. As agreed, the Danes wintered on the Humber, and 'took a large quantity of treasure on board and kept the chief men (of York) in bonds'. Perhaps in accumulating this treasure, like their successors at Ely, they had achieved the purpose of their expedition. But although William had agreed to allow them to live off the countryside, in practice he permitted nothing of the sort. That winter, as William also found to his cost, was an especially harsh one. The Danes, prevented from foraging by the close watch kept on them, suffered many deaths from the cold and the same lack of food as affected the citizens of Yorkshire. They could only watch helplessly while William turned Yorkshire into a wasteland. Few survived, demoralised and half-starving, to return in spring to Denmark. Breaking with his newly established tradition, William, in a show intended to overawe the thegns of the region, held his Christmas crown-wearing at York, sending to Winchester for the regalia. The castles were rebuilt and Norman control over Yorkshire fully asserted. Despite the Aetheling and his men being still at large somewhere, certain of local support, there was really no native army capable of capturing castles in York. To this extent the harrying of the North was to be a success. The English had dispersed into the woods and marshes in small groups, returning to their role as *silvatici*. William could not leave this situation as it was – he needed to end the last significant threat, as he then saw it, to his hold on the crown of England. He decided to hunt out and kill as many as possible and wipe out their hiding places. In doing so he also attacked the unprotected and defenceless peasantry, creating a wasteland between York and Durham.

Without waiting for the end of winter William ordered a thorough search to be made for the wildmen, village by village, even into the forests and hills. He also ordered the complete devastation of the region. Some of the rebels, including in their number the Aetheling, had sought refuge in an isolated part of the lower Tees valley north of York, an inaccessible site where they had stored some supplies. William, possibly informed of their whereabouts, marched after them despite the difficulties of the terrain and the weather. Orderic describes him 'forcing his way through the trackless wastes, over ground so rough that he was frequently compelled to go on foot'. He penetrated into 'a narrow neck of land sheltered on all sides by the sea or marshes. It could only be reached by a narrow causeway, no more than 20ft wide.' Exactly where this was is still a problem. Orderic actually says '*in angulo quodam regionis*', in a certain corner of the province, which suggests Holderness which was almost an island in 1070, cut off by the marshes of the River Hull and accessible only from Skipsea. Wherever it was, when he got there, the enemy had gone.

If Simeon of Durham is right in his account, Malcolm made matters worse shortly after the Danes had left by raiding Cospatrick's lands. The *Historia Regum* says that Malcolm met Edgar at Wearmouth before Cospatrick's raid on Edenvale and 'during the Scots' pillaging and wasting, Earl Cospatrick went into Cumberland'. Caught between William and the Scots, Cospatrick made his submission.

William remained north for some time, receiving the renewed submission of Waltheof and, by messenger, of Cospatrick. Surely the fact that he was prepared to do so shows that he had little hope of depriving Cospatrick of power in the North or of controlling Northumbria without the assistance of the two earls. The York castles were to be the de facto limits of William's authority. He could not play the old game and use the men of York as a check on the Northumbrians. The king had to recognise Cospatrick and the House of Bamburgh, accepting an offer of submission, which the earl wisely made by proxy, not wishing to come within William's grasp, and even install Waltheof as earl; but the dark side of this was that it left the Northumbrians to face the Scots alone, and that explains, in part at least, William's invasion of Scotland in 1072, a delayed response to King Malcolm's harrying of Teesdale in 1070. Cospatrick's earldom, forfeited in 1068, was now restored to him, although he remained in exile in Scotland. The restoration of the earldom upset Malcolm enough to cause a local war. Malcolm's men were permitted to harry Cospatrick's territory on the north-east coast and the earl in his turn raided in Edenvale and the Solway Plain. William was able to seize his opportunity and invaded Scotland by both land and sea and imposed the Treaty of Abernethy (1072) on Malcolm.

While in the North King William 'continued to comb forests and remote mountainous places, stopping at nothing to hunt out the enemy hidden there'. Edgar had retreated to Scotland and made no sign. He had been stripped of his honours by William after he had originally gone to Scotland in 1068.

For his return march, William had chosen a particularly harsh and hazardous route, difficult for men and horses, following a route described as one no army had hitherto attempted, between towering peaks and precipitous valleys deep in snow. Thus he returned from the vicinity of Hexham to the Tees and on to York which was now separated from Durham by a fifty-mile *cordon sanitaire* of devastation. From there he set out to deal once and for all with the rebels in Cheshire. He had done his best to destroy the native society of Yorkshire so that it would no longer provide a base for a future Danish attack. Thus the royal demesne was bloated with confiscated estates which were then used to support the setting up of a sheriff over the whole area, while the 'earldom' of Yorkshire was suppressed. This explains why King Swein's next venture was in the Fens. The Danes still dreamed of plundering England and over the ensuing decades some even tried it. They took York in 1075 (after the failure of the Revolt of the Earls) and again in 1085 and even prepared an expeditionary force in 1070 which brought Swein of Denmark to the Humber in violation of Osbjorn's agreement with William. The men of York, mere months after the harrying, were still ready to support a Danish invader. But William was now both feared and powerful.

The rebels and their Danish allies refused to meet William in the field. This was mainly a result of the northern concept of warfare, to which men like Cospatrick were well accustomed. This was to use rural ambushes and raids, and surprise attacks; tactics seen by the Normans as treacherous. No invader had been able to stay long in the North and when the enemy had left, the thegns hiding in the woods and hills would emerge to take up the struggle once again. Furthermore, the Normans in York had proved just as rapacious as de Commines and the castle there had amassed a great treasure when thegns were imprisoned and estates confiscated. This treasure may well have been one of the objectives of the Yorkshire thegns in 1069. The Chroniclers saw William's tactics in 1068 as successful, but that success had been only a partial one. He had taken York, stayed eight days, and built a second castle, but there had been no political settlement. The North was still in revolt.

As they had always done, the leaders went to the hills and waited for William to leave and in the following year the war had been renewed, this time with the assistance of the Danes. Now William's policy was different. The harrying was intended to put an end to trouble in the North by eliminating not only the hiding places but also the means of subsistence of the rebels. Leaving his lieutenants to complete the devastation, the king turned to deal with the remnants of the rebellion in Cheshire.

William took the most difficult and perilous way across harsh mountainous tracks. Some of the army began to grumble about the conditions of the march, which were of a kind to which they were not accustomed. These were the men from Anjou, Brittany and Maine. For them the cold meant much suffering and the death of many horses. They therefore asked to be released from the terms which they had accepted when given their fiefs but William refused to bargain. Setting an example of endurance himself, he appealed to the loyalty of his Normans, and led his men to Chester.

Here William found, as so often elsewhere, that his mere presence with an army was enough to quell all resistance. He built a castle at Chester and another at Stafford and inflicted on the area the same wasting and ravaging as had already been carried out in Yorkshire and Durham, laying waste in Cheshire over 100 manors. He then returned to Salisbury where he dismissed the bulk of his army after congratulating them on their achievements and distributing rewards. But those who had caused trouble were retained for another forty days' service in the field. The culmination was another crown-wearing in full court at Winchester at which Waltheof was required to renew his submission in a public ceremony. So by the spring of 1070, by force of arms and his own prestige, and above all by a policy of unremitting wholesale terror, William had imposed his will and Norman rule on the North.

The whole kingdom was now his, from Northumbria to the Channel and from the North Sea to Wales and the Irish Sea. The sources refer to this period as the time when William took pride in the 'kingdom which he had recently acquired'. William, who had twice blundered in his appointment of men to rule the North, had now saved himself by a policy of genocide. In the North, as elsewhere, he carried out a deliberate and ruthless policy of terror, mutilation of hostages and devastation of arable land. Permanent problems remained. Trouble never really came to an end. The benefactors of Selby, only ten miles from York, were harassed by outlaws and Hugh fitzBaldric, the sheriff, needed a small army as escort whenever he travelled because of the continued hostility of the English. The monks of Whitby were to complain of trouble from outlaws as late as the reign of William Rufus and 'brigand-age' remained a problem as disinherited thegns became outlaws. In the whole southern end of the Pennines into Derbyshire and Staffordshire Norman power was not fully established until the end of William's reign. In practice Norman rule was restricted to the eastern and western coastal plains and in between all was brigandage and out-lawry while the North remained violent and unstable. This explains the vital importance of Tutbury and Nottingham castles, held by Henry of Ferrers and William Peverel respectively. It is curious in the light of this that in Geoffrey Gaimar's account of Hereward he is said to have been killed by knights from *Estutesberie*, that is Tutbury.

THE HARRYING OF THE NORTH

There remains a stain on William's honour and reputation, and that is 'the harrying of the North'. Having ordered the seeking out and destruction of all rebels, William then inflicted the most dreadful suffering on the unfortunate population. Yet some historians have tried to play down the impact of the harrying, arguing that it was not judged by the writers of the *Anglo-Saxon Chronicle* as harshly as they had judged the Danish ravaging in 1006. Some suggest that not all entries of 'waste' recorded in 1086 were due to action by the Norman army. Some entries of 'waste' no doubt were due to the absence of information which led the Domesday scribes to write 'waste' because they had nothing else to say, and some places may have already been waste in 1066. Some entries could have been the result of changes in methods of cultivation introduced by the new Norman lords in search of greater profits.

There is some force in these arguments but too much must not be read into variations in the words used by the Chroniclers to describe similar events. The *Chronicles* were kept in abbeys and were open to inspection by visitors, lay and ecclesiastical, so records would have been toned down if written within the lifetime of participants in the events recorded. It should be remembered that the Old English monarchy, as the *Leges Henrici Primi* record, knew of a capital offence of slander against the king's person and that 'whoever despises or speaks ill of him' shall be put in the royal mercy. The accounts of later writers like 'Florence' of Worcester, Orderic Vitalis and Simeon of Durham, are far more critical and use far harsher language, spelling out the consequences of the harrying. The two versions of the *Anglo-Saxon Chronicle*, labelled (D) and (E), were written up for this period at Worcester, under St Wulfstan, and at St Augustine's, Canterbury, where Lanfranc was archbishop.

We do not have William of Poitiers' account, as the end of his History is lost, but Orderic Vitalis had seen and used it and it probably contained information which forms the basis of Orderic's account. As for William of Jumièges, his account is careful to pass over the harrying as he ends his work with the restoration of peace in England. The Chroniclers' accounts are definite in themselves. (D) says, 'he marched northward with all the levies he could muster, and plundered and utterly laid waste that shire' and (E), 'King William marched into that shire and completely devastated it'. Then 'Florence' says;

> He at once assembled his army, and hastening with an angry heart into Northumbria, ceased not during the whole winter to lay waste the land, to murder the inhabitants and inflict numerous injuries.

True, he then lays some of the blame on 'the Northmen', but he says that the destruction was confined to Northumbria in 1069 and extended to the whole of Mercia in 1070 and was most severe in the North, with the result that 'so great a famine prevailed that men were forced to consume the flesh of horses, dogs, cats and even human beings'. Orderic Vitalis, brought up in Shropshire where he would have heard tales of the campaign, and acquainted with the lost ending of William of Poitiers' work, says that William had never before shown such cruelty and that he made no effort to restrain his fury nor to prevent the punishment of the innocent along with the guilty. In his anger he had ordered both the harvest and all the beasts to be reduced to ashes and all reserves of food destroyed. So the whole region north of the Humber was deprived of the means of subsistence.

Orderic, like Florence, insists that there was a serious shortage of food over all England in 1070 as a result of William's actions and that the humble and defenceless population suffered such famine that 100,000 men and women, both old and young, died because of it. The figure given, like all such medieval estimates, means only a very great number. But Hugh the Chantor at York and William of Malmesbury in his *De Gestis Regum* support Orderic's account, claiming that large areas were destroyed by famine and the sword, as does the *Historia Regum*, usually attributed to Simeon of Durham.

William of Malmesbury speaks of the wholesale destruction of Yorkshire, the county previously so fertile, given over to fire, plunder and bloodshed and left uncultivated even to his own times. Half the vills of the North Riding and over one third of those of the East and West Ridings were wholly or partially wasted. This cannot be explained away by scribal ignorance or Norman farming methods. The conclusion is that the harrying had been both thorough and merciless and the accounts of it cannot be dismissed as rhetorical exaggeration. Nor would it have mattered to the poor unfortunate peasantry who was ultimately responsible for their plight, the Northmen or the Normans.

The most compelling verdict on the harrying comes in Orderic's deathbed speech attributed by him to the Conqueror. This was composed on the Classical model as found in Roman authors such as Livy. Readers would have understood the convention by which such speeches become a vehicle for the writer's own views of what might have been said. Orderic puts the following words into William's own mouth:

> I have persecuted the native inhabitants beyond all reason…
> I have cruelly oppressed them; many unjustly disinherited;
> innumerable multitudes, especially in the County of York,
> perished through me by famine or the sword. I fell upon
> the English of the Northern Shires like a ravening lion. I
> commanded their houses and corn and all their implements
> and chattels to be burnt without distinction, and large herds
> of cattle and beasts of burden to be butchered wherever they
> were found. It was then that I took revenge on multitudes
> of both sexes by subjecting them to the calamity of cruel
> famine. I became the barbarous murderer of many thousands
> both young and old. Having therefore made my way to the
> throne of that Kingdom by so many crimes, I dare not leave
> it to anyone but God.

6

The Sack of
Peterborough

Having dismissed his army at Salisbury on his return
from the North, William held his Easter Court of
1070 at Westminster. He then proceeded to take
action in a great council at Winchester to confirm his power,
'in a kingdom he had but newly acquired' (Florence) by
depriving 'certain persons', namely bishops and abbots, of
their positions and honours 'without their being guilty of
any open crime' and imprisoned them for life. This was
done, says Florence again, 'solely by mistrust of losing his
newly acquired kingdom'. This left the other bishops trembling in anticipation of the loss of their own honours. This
account does suggest that William realised that the rebellion
in the North had been a very dangerous one and that he
might easily have been defeated. That phrase used twice

by Florence of Worcester, about William's 'newly acquired' kingdom, suggests that the Chronicler did not regard the kingdom as fully won by William until after the defeat of the northern rebellion.

Events immediately after this remain somewhat obscure, especially the movements of the Danish fleet which had been expected, in accordance with its agreement with the king, to return to Denmark. It appears that Swein Estrithson of Denmark now took a hand in person. Sometime in the spring of 1070 he arrived off the Humber and ordered his fleet to break the agreement and instead move down to The Wash and into the Ouse, intending to set up a base at Ely.

Once there, the Danes joined forces with the outlawed Lincolnshire thegn Hereward. This man is introduced into the account of the year 1070 in the *Anglo-Saxon Chronicle* in exactly the same manner as other prominent men are introduced, as though the reader will know immediately who he is. When he is mentioned he has already risen to a position of leadership. Hereward and his *genge* (variously rendered by translators as gang, band or company) then joined the Danes in an attack on Peterborough Abbey, an attack which took place apparently in late spring 1071. Details of the attack are given in the Peterborough version of the *Chronicle* and by Hugh Candidus in his *History of the Abbey*. After the attack the Danes did not, as the English had hoped, persist in their incursion but returned to Denmark, leaving Hereward and his followers to maintain a desperate last stand against King William.

If that were all there was to this affair it would be of little significance, but on reflection it can be seen to be a more serious matter than first appears. There is the fact that after the Danes had left, Hereward was joined at Ely by the remaining disaffected English magnates. A number had already been reconciled to King William after renewing their submission, such as Earl Waltheof and Cospatrick, and others had taken refuge in Scotland with the Aetheling and his family. But Earl Morcar, accompanied according to some accounts by his brother Earl Edwin, together with Bishop Aethelwine of Durham, the prominent thegn Siward Barn, and a number of others, with a large following of supporters, joined the rebels in Ely.

In consequence of these reinforcements, Hereward was now able to carry on with his guerrilla warfare against the Normans in the Fens, until the defenders in the isle were eventually induced to surrender on the basis of false prom-ises of reconciliation by King William. Hereward escaped, leading a small band of his own men to relative safety in the forested area known as the Brunneswald. There he contin-ued to live an outlaw existence, like those other opponents of the king, the *silvatici*. Thereafter, accounts of this man become inextricably bound up with a great deal of legend-ary material aimed at painting him as some sort of leader of a national Resistance movement, though we know he only came on the scene towards the end. His deeds are related mainly as a means of recovering for the English a reputation for military ability and knightly prowess.

The career and legend of Hereward illustrate for us the kind of guerrilla warfare to which the English had been compelled to resort. His ultimate end is shrouded in mystery, with two conflicting versions now current, neither of which can be true.

These last stages of the English revolt, as described so far, may seem of little account. Yet there are aspects of the affair which invite a closer look. It might well be asked why it was that what looks, as described by the *Chronicles*, like the desperate last stand of a comparatively small group of out-laws, should have required the personal intervention of King William, with the consequent expenditure of time, effort and lives, including the employment of a land army and a fleet, at a time when affairs in Normandy and Maine demanded his attention. The role of the Danes needs further examina-tion and some explanation must be provided for Hereward's attack on Peterborough. After all, one of the most solid facts about him is that he was the 'man' of the abbey, with obligations towards it and holding lands from it.

In considering the nature and course of the king's attack on Ely, the twefth-century accounts found in the *Liber Eliensis* or Ely Book are most useful, especially when taken with the text of the *De Gestis Herewardi*, in illustrating the nature of the guerrilla warfare fought by those who had taken refuge on the isle. Something must have been the cause of Hereward's actions and the decision of the magnates to flee. The first factor lies in a report found in the *Anglo-Saxon Chronicle* for 1070 which says that King William 'had all the monasteries that were in England plundered'.

This bare statement is expanded by 'Florence' of Worcester and Gervase of Canterbury (who wrote under Richard I and John). Gervase says that William I had all the charters and moveable property of the English monasteries seized in 1070. If this is so, it goes some way towards explaining why so many charters were produced and incorporated in *Chronicles* and cartularies in the period after 1071, either in the form of copies of originals or of forged or interpolated versions of missing originals. It should be remembered that not all medieval 'forged' or 'spurious' charters are presenting entirely false claims. They may not be original, and can be shown to be full of errors, but often represent an attempt to recreate a missing document or to provide written proof of what was originally a verbal gift or agreement. It also throws light on Orderic's report about Odo of Bayeux, that the monasteries complained that he 'violently and unjustly' robbed them 'of the ancient endowments given them by pious Englishmen'.

Florence's story is quite detailed. He says that King William acted on the advice of William, Earl of Hereford and certain (unnamed) others, and had all the monasteries searched, ordering that: 'all the money which the wealthiest of the English had deposited in them on account of the plundering of the land, should be removed and placed in his Treasury'.

On the face of it, that was barefaced robbery. Much of this wealth was thus not monastic property, but it would seem that those who carried out the king's orders were none too particular about distinguishing the monks' property from that of their depositors. In the eleventh century there were no banks or safety deposits. So the safest place to store your money and valuables was a monastery, left in the keeping of the abbot and trusting in respect for the Church to protect them. It is surely significant that this seems to have been the occasion of the decision of the two earls to leave court, probably early in 1071, and join the last rebels. It is conceivable that some of their wealth had been confiscated in this way or that they decided to withdraw it and flee the country with it. Thus robbery could be part of the motive behind the mysterious fate of Earl Edwin.

Certainly the decision to confiscate the wealth of English thegns held by the monasteries would have rendered many surviving thegns both destitute and desperate. There is no hint that it was applied only to the wealth of those who were dead, though in that case it would be an early example of punitive death duties, and it completed the expropriation of the thegns who had already lost their lands. If it applied also to those thegns who had survived or to the heirs of the dead, it explains their desperation. Nor can it have helped that this was done in the year of the great famine. Orderic again points the moral; 'So foreigners grew wealthy with the spoils of England while her own sons were either shamefully slain or driven as exiles to wander hopelessly through foreign kingdoms'.

One of those foreign kingdoms was Denmark and into this situation there then entered King Swein of Denmark, seeking no doubt to capitalise on it for his own advantage. The *Chronicle*'s version of events has some significant aspects. It says that at King Swein's arrival on the Humber:

the people of the countryside met him and came to terms with him, thinking that he was sure to conquer the whole country. He had with him Earl Osbjorn and Bishop Christian of Aarhus and the Danish huscarls and he went to Ely where Englishmen from all the Fenlands came to meet them, thinking that they were sure to conquer the whole land.

This was a significant movement involving a considerable body of men. The *Chronicle* emphasises the point by repeating itself in almost identical words.

At this stage it appears that Hereward and his men took on a significant role. The *Chronicle* says that the Peterborough monks had now heard that 'their own men, namely Hereward and his band' wished to plunder the monastery and that this was to be done to prevent the wealth of the abbey falling into the hands of a French abbot.

Much of this story is found also in the *History of Peterborough Abbey* by Hugh Candidus, who gives additional information about the nature of the items taken by the outlaw force, such as the gold diadem from the Great Crucifix and its gold footrest from the feet of the Crucified, the altar-frontal of gold and silver (which was hidden in the tower), gold and silver reliquaries and crosses together with money, vestments and books.

Hereward's men (or Hereward himself according to Hugh Candidus) insisted that they were doing this out of loyalty to the monastery, to keep its belongings out of Norman hands. Nonetheless, one of the monks, called Yware (Ivar) tried to forestall the removal of the treasure by taking what he could of the gospel books and robes and handing them over to the new abbot. He removed only items of relatively little importance. He may have been trying to curry favour with the new man but if so, he chose a strange way of doing so. He was later reported to have tried to recover some of the lost items from Denmark, especially the relics of saints.

The sources have a dramatic account of an attack by way of the Bolhithe gate at the east end of the abbey, which opened onto a landing-stage or *hythe*, and the use of fire by the outlaws which destroyed the monastery and the houses of the unfortunate peasantry round about it, leaving only the church and possibly the infirmary. This account comes mainly from Peterborough itself, as version (E) of the *Anglo-Saxon Chronicle* was written up there after 1121 (after a fire had destroyed the library) using a copy borrowed from St Augustine's, Canterbury. Local information was added to the text by the copyists.

The reason for Hereward's action is to be found in the circumstances surrounding the appointment of the new abbot. After the death of the pre-Conquest abbot, Leofric (a relative of Leofric, Earl of Mercia) following his return from the Battle of Hastings, the monks had elected Brand their provost. He then made the mistake of approaching the Aetheling, Edgar, for recognition as abbot, and the prince was only too glad to oblige. King William was enraged by this and was only persuaded to accept Brand by the efforts of intermediaries and the payment of a heavy fine. Abbot Brand only lived for three years after his election, dying on 27 November 1069. William then decided that the strategic position of Peterborough at the gateway to the Fens required the appointment of a Norman. He chose a monk of Fécamp, at the time ruling Malmesbury Abbey, called Turold (O.N. Thoraldr). He had proved too tyrannical for the Malmesbury monks and William of Malmesbury relates that when he was chosen by King William, the king had remarked that since he behaved more like a soldier than a monk, he would give him someone to fight. William of Malmesbury simply records the transfer of Turold to Peterborough, commenting that 'this was disturbed, being infested with brigands led by a certain Hereward who was located among the marshes.'

Hereward, acting with the assistance of the Danes, had therefore decided to strike before the Norman arrived as he was reported to have an escort of knights. This was a force of about 160 knights, a number large enough to be regarded as a small army, perhaps given him by King William. Hereward had persuaded the Danes that there were rich pickings to be obtained from the abbey, and took the view that it was better to destroy it than let Turold have it intact. The Danes, aided by Hereward and his men, attacked the abbey in small boats and when at first repelled set fire to the 'vill', the street of houses alongside the abbey and the Bolhithe gate which provided access to the enclosure, and so entered the abbey. Turold arrived after the outlaws had gone to find it a smoking ruin. He was to exploit the lands of the abbey and rebuild it according to Norman ideas.

The connection between Hereward and Peterborough went rather deeper than one might expect. He is described as a 'man' of the abbey and was certainly its tenant, possibly holding lands on a life tenancy. He would, therefore, have been 'commended' to the abbot, accepting him as his lord. The original arrangement had probably been made with Abbot Leofric and may have been renewed by Abbot Brand. There is a story in the *Gesta Herewardi* that Hereward had approached Abbot Brand and asked to be made a knight and that the abbot had knighted him. This would have occurred in 1067 or 1068 after Hereward's return to England. It reflects twelfth-century understanding of eleventh-century actions. As it stands the story is untenable. There is no evidence of Anglo-Saxon abbots dubbing thegns to knighthood and thegns in good standing would not have expected it. We know that King Harold during his sojourn in William's hands in Normandy had accepted arms and armour from the duke, an action interpreted by the Normans as his becoming the 'man' of the duke, but this was clearly a Norman not an English custom. To writers in the twelfth century 'commendation' might well have been seen as a dubbing ceremony.

That Hereward was the 'man' of the monks explains his fury at the appointment of a Norman abbot. Nor was Turold's

appointment welcome to the monks. This is perhaps illustrated by the fact that when Turold died the brethren elected
Godric, Brand's youngest brother, as abbot. Unfortunately
he did not hold office for long. He was deposed by a Synod
presided over by Archbishop Anselm on the grounds, rather
unfairly, of simony, because the monks had been obliged
to pay a considerable sum of money to William Rufus for
confirmation of the election, but probably in reality because
he was an Englishman.

After the attack on the abbey, Hereward and his men and
their Danish allies returned to the Isle of Ely by boat, taking
with them the abbey treasure which Hereward, unwisely
perhaps, entrusted to the Danes for safe keeping. The monks
who wrote about these events naturally saw this as the action
of an outlaw. William of Malmesbury regarded Hereward
as a small-time robber, a *latrunculus*. Hugh Candidus says
that Hereward had persuaded the Danes to take part in the
attack by describing the abbey's wealth, and calls his men
'malefactors'. Yet he has to admit that Hereward was the
abbey's man, owing service to it.

From Hereward's point of view the affair ended disas-
trously. The Danes took the treasure aboard their ships, and
when Swein did a deal with King William and agreed, at
a price, to return to Denmark, they took the treasure with
them, as well as a number of Peterborough monks led by
their prior, Athelwold. Unfortunately for the Danes, their
fleet was overwhelmed by a great storm and scattered, some
ending up in Norway or Ireland and the rest limping back
to Denmark.

There, we are told, even the church in which the
Peterborough goods were stored burnt down through the
Danes' own drunken carelessness. Hugh Candidus claims
that Prior Athelwold and his monks managed to rescue
the Arm of St Oswald and other relics which, after the
monks had been released, were sent to Ramsey Abbey
for safety. From there they were eventually restored to

1 Eleventh-century kings of England – portraits based on coinage of their times but in a Victorian cameo presentation.

Above & right: 2 & 3
Norman ships, from
the Bayeux Tapestry.

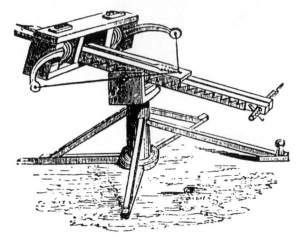

4 Balista weapon,
for throwing
darts, stones etc.
Resembles a cross-
bow, but much
larger and stronger.

5 Devil's Dyke between Reach and Burwell, Cambridgeshire.

6 Fen Water Meadow, near Upware, Cambridgeshire.

Left: 7 St Mary Magdalene's Church, Campsall, South Yorkshire, illustrating the Saxon tower with Norman additions.

Below left: 8 A Saxon doorway, St Mary Magdalene's Church, Campsall.

Below right: 9 Banner of St Etheldreda, Ely Cathedral.

Above: 10 Juxtaposition of a Saxon window with decorated Norman archway above it (right), with an early English (gothic) window (left), St Mary Magdalene's Church, Campsall.

Left: 11 Fortifiable round tower of St Mary's Church, Burnham Deepdale, Norfolk.

Below: 12 Castle Acre, Norfolk showing the motte and the ditch.

13, 14 & 15 Wicken Fen. These three photographs show how little the landscape has changed since the eleventh century and illustrate the conditions both the rebels and their pursuers had to contend with.

Peterborough, but only after Turold had threatened to burn down Ramsey.

Turold had arrived at Peterborough after the attack was over. Only one monk was there to meet him, Leofwine the Tall, who had been ill in the infirmary and unable to leave with the others. Such monks as had not chosen to go with the outlaws had scattered into the surrounding countryside, and they now gradually returned. Within a week services could again be held in the church which was undamaged. Over the next few years the abbey was rebuilt. Turold decided that he would not be defeated by any future attack and built a castle, called Mount Turold, right next door to the abbey. He also took possession of many of the surviving ornaments and the lands of the monastery.

When King William imposed military service on all the southern abbeys (probably sometime around 1070-1072), Peterborough, not only because of its extensive lands but also because of its strategic position, was assigned a quota (the *Servicium Debitum*) of sixty knights, higher than any other except Ely (which had an equally large punitive quota imposed on it because of its rebellion).

Turold was one of the first abbots to move his knights out of monastery precincts. Some formed the garrison of his castle and the others were provided with fiefs carved out of the abbey demesne. Hugh Candidus asserts that he gave land to the knights he had brought with him and to his relatives so that scarcely a third of the abbey's lands remained in the demesne. Domesday Book records some thirty unnamed *milites*, that is knights, holding small estates under Turold and about fifteen named tenants with mainly Norman names. Other evidence reveals that Hugh Candidus was exaggerating the loss of land. The additions to Hugh's text made by Walter of Whittlesey in the thirteenth century claim that he created fiefs for sixty knights but this looks like a deduction from the known figure of sixty knights as the abbey quota.

The building of a castle and the sub-infeudation of knights on abbey lands is also confirmed by the fourteenth-century *Annales Burgo-Spaldenses* (also called the *Chronicle of Abbot John*) in an obituary notice on Turold who died in 1098. He is said to have distributed sixty-two hides of land to his stipendiary knights who gave him protection against 'Hereward le Wake' (one of the earliest uses of this phrase).

Neither Turold nor the monks of Peterborough could have been expected to forgive Hereward's action in robbing the monastery and this is proved by the retreat of Hereward and the other Peterborough tenants who were with him to their refuge on the Isle of Ely. They had no option now but to hold out there, having been deserted by the Danes. The events that then followed at Ely are recorded in the *Liber Eliensis* and the *Gesta Herewardi*, and summarised in the major *Chronicles*. To work out a comprehensible account of the siege of Ely requires careful evaluation of the sources and the separation of much fiction from the real facts.

One tradition, found in Geoffrey Gaimar's *L'Estorie des Engles*, claims that the attack on Peterborough came after the siege when Hereward and his men were in the Brunneswald. As this is contrary to the account in the major sources it cannot be accepted as it stands. It must be a much embroidered story based on Hereward's activities while at Ely in 1070–71 and consists of an exaggerated account of minor skirmishes between Hereward and his Norman opponents. Much of it, such as the capture and ransoming of Turold, is the stuff of twelfth-century romance. The attack on the abbey is also misplaced in the *Liber Eliensis* and that reveals how poor was the compiler's understanding of his sources.

A final fact about the 'sack' of Peterborough is that it was never a random act of vandalism. The church was not destroyed and services resumed in it shortly after Turold's arrival. The treasure, as we have seen, was not shared out among the outlaws but stored at Ely, only to be taken out of the country when the Danes fled back to their homeland.

No monk was harmed, not even those taken to Ely and then Denmark with the treasure, and Hereward ordered the return of all hostages (which probably gave rise to the idea that he captured Turold and released him for a ransom). Hereward's quarrel was always with the Normans rather than with the monks.

If Edwin as well as Morcar joined Hereward at Ely he did not stay long. Both brothers had fled from King William's court together, some six months earlier, moved by disenchantment to make what proved to be a final break. They had still been at court for Queen Matilda's coronation in May 1068 but had watched with increasing dismay as the Normans grew rich at English expense. Orderic insists on Edwin's disappointment when his promised marriage showed no sign of materialising and Morcar had been slighted when William appointed first Copsige and then Cospatrick to rule Northumbria. Edwin also no doubt resented the authority given to Abbot Aethelwig of Evesham within Mercia, believing he should have been consulted, especially as Evesham had been favoured by the Earls of Mercia in earlier times. In 1068 Edwin, like his father Aelfgar, turned to the Welsh for aid, allying with Bleddyn of Gwynedd, the associate of Eadric the Wild. The two earls played a leading part in the abortive rising of 1068, hastily dispersing their men at William's approach. During the Great Rising of 1069–70 the earls had preferred a watching brief, awaiting the outcome, though Edwin might well have been in touch with his men in Cheshire and Staffordshire who were involved.

Some time after the attack on Peterborough in 1070, by Hereward and the Danes, the earls picked their moment to slip away from William's court, aware, it is said, of rumours that he intended to imprison them. They then wandered 'in woods and fields' for some time, having gone *silvaticus*. Geoffrey Gaimar says that they met Bishop Aethelwine of Durham and Siward Barn, with other disaffected Englishmen, making their way to Ely, intending to overwinter there before seeking exile. They met at '*Welle*', which probably means the Wellstream (or Wisbech Ouse) near Peterborough, joining the Nene River at Upwell and running through Outwell to the Ouse, which explains the Ely belief that both earls came to the abbey.

Edwin parted company from his brother almost immediately, either on arrival at Ely or perhaps a little earlier, preferring to travel north to seek help in Scotland. Orderic puts what happened next after the fall of Ely, but this contradicts all other sources and he might have done this for dramatic effect, to support his unfounded belief that Edwin tried to rescue Morcar from his prison. *The Worcester Chronicle* (D) has Edwin killed before Morcar goes to Ely and the (E) version, from Peterborough, reverses the order, suggesting either that these events were more or less simultaneous or that no one knew which came first. *The Liber Eliensis*, using one of its unknown sources, believed that Edwin was at Ely throughout the siege by King William, despite citing information from Florence of Worcester about Edwin's decision to seek out King Malcolm in Scotland. The Peterborough text (E) says that Edwin was killed 'treacherously' and both versions of the *Chronicle* say that it was at the hands of some of his own men. Florence of Worcester expands on this, relating that Edwin was killed, after deciding to seek King Malcolm's aid, 'in an ambush laid by his own people'. Orderic has the fullest account. He claims that the earl was trapped on the banks of a river by the rising tide, betrayed by three brothers who were his servants, and died fighting desperately to the last with twenty of his men. It has been suggested that Orderic was using an epic poem about the fall of the earls. He may well have encountered something like that during his visits to several fenland monasteries to collect information. Morcar remained at Ely where he would certainly have been the ranking magnate present. Possibly he commanded the overall defence while Hereward and his men carried out raids and foraging expeditions.

7

The Siege of Ely

The *Anglo-Saxon Chronicle* for the year 1070 insists on the welcome given to the Danes after the arrival of King Swein and the expectation of the Fenmen that the Danes would expel the Normans and conquer the country. It is this reaction which explains King William's decision to make an end of rebellion once and for all by dealing with the problem of Ely. At first he was content to deal with the Danish threat as he had done earlier by offering them money to persuade them to leave without a fight. He obviously realised that their only aim was to get rich quick and that they were unwilling to face a Norman army equipped with cavalry. Swein was only too ready to accept the bribe and leave, taking with him the booty seized at Peterborough. William doubtless thought the English rebels would leave with the Danes.

The preliminary part of William's strategy had been to send Abbot Turold to take control of the monastery at

Peterborough, equipped with a useful force of knights. Unfortunately for the Normans, Hereward had persuaded the Danes to raid the abbey and this was carried out just before Turold's arrival, while the Norman was at Stamford. The new abbot was now fully occupied in restoring the abbey. Any further action would require William's own participation.

For the rest of 1070 Hereward and his men remained at Ely and nothing is known directly of any activity on their part, though we may surmise that time was spent in fortifying the abbey against any future attack and, as the *Liber Eliensis* insists, 'pillaging far and wide'. Some of the stories of Hereward's struggles against various Normans while an outlaw in the Brunneswald could actually apply to the period between the attack on Peterborough and the decision of the king to deal with Ely once and for all or even to Hereward's sojourn 'in the marshes' during 1069. The tales have Hereward opposing several prominent local Norman magnates. He is the enemy of Ivo Taillebois, Sheriff of Lincolnshire, against whom he fights near Stamford. Abbot Turold and his men are also involved. Another opponent was Ogier the Breton, the new Lord of Bourne, who had taken over several of the estates previously held by Hereward. At some time during 1070 Hereward is reported to have ambushed and killed Frederick of Oosterzele-Scheldewindeke, the brother-in-law of William of Warenne, later Earl of Surrey. The slaying earned Hereward the undying enmity of Earl William. Another whose name is linked with that of Hereward is Gilbert of Ghent. The sources claim they met before 1066 in Northumbria. However, Gilbert is not known to have been in England before the Conquest. Any first encounter would have been more likely to have taken place in Flanders, as an attempt to persuade Hereward to accept knighthood from Gilbert would make more sense in that context. Some of Gilbert's lands were in Lincolnshire where he was the successor of Ulf Fenisc, especially at Witham-on-the-Hill and Manthorpe as well as Barholme and Stow, places associated with Hereward. He, too, would have attracted attention in 1070. The *Liber Eliensis* also mentions 'Gilbert of Clare', which surely refers to the Suffolk baron Richard fitzGilbert of Clare. Lastly there is William Malet, a prominent lieutenant of the Conqueror, one of the defenders of York. Several charters of this period are dated ominously as being given 'when William Malet went into the marsh' and presumably died there.

As for Hereward and his men, they bound themselves in a solemn agreement to defend the Isle of Ely and the shrine of St Etheldreda, requiring all who joined them to swear oaths over the tomb of the saint, invoking her protection. The saint thus became the patroness of a political movement. Then the situation changed. In the autumn of 1071 the Earls Edwin and Morcar arrived at Ely, by way of 'Welle', or so the *Liber Eliensis* insists, accompanied by Bishop Aethelwine of Durham, brother of Bishop Aethelric, as well as the prominent Danelaw thegn Siward Barn or Bearn, together with a number of other nobles (*proceres*) and a large body of their supporters. This, for William, put a different complexion on the affair and he took decisive action, summoning both a land army and a fleet and launching an attack on the isle.

He found himself faced with an appalling task, one he had never attempted before. Ely at this time was almost literally an island, surrounded on all sides either by deep rivers or by even deeper morasses. It was as the *Liber Eliensis* says, 'Beset by a great mere and fens as though by a strong wall.' It extended at its maximum boundaries from 'Cotingelade' (a lode or waterway near Cottenham) to Littleport or Abbotsdelf and from Stretham Mere to Chirchewere (probably near Sutton). The monks said it was seven miles by four miles in extent but modern measures give twelve by ten; medieval measures of distance are almost always underestimated. Later accounts speak of four points of entry, at Littleport, Stuntney, Earith and Aldreth, but in the mid-eleventh century only Aldreth was at all useful. The breadth of the fen there was said to be four furlongs but in fact was nearer to sixteen, that is two miles which is also the length of King William's causeway as given by Florence of Worcester. It is worth remembering that the fenland consisted of undrained swamp with meandering tributaries of the Ouse running through it and contained small islands often supporting single villages, such as Stuntney or Coveney, and larger islands capable of being farmed. The largest island was Ely itself. The isle was not cut off from the sea but access to it elsewhere was prevented by almost stagnant meres and marshes. The *Liber Eliensis* says it had at one time been usual to go there by boat but had become too dangerous for that. After the siege, says the *Liber Eliensis*, 'a causeway has now been made through the marshy sedge-bank and it is possible to go there on foot'. This account is confirmed by the *Gesta Stephani* which also speaks of 'a narrow track' which 'affords the scantiest of entries' and by a reference to a causeway in one of the Conqueror's writs of 1082.

The Fenland (Archaeological) Survey has shown that the land between Aldreth and Ely consisted of a number of islands connected by causeways, that is, trackways of gravelly flint, connecting villages such as Witchford and Coveney or Wardy Hill. Following such a route brings one out at West Fen on the western side of Ely where, in the mid-eleventh century, the actual town of Ely was located on the sloping ground running up to the site of the monastery which lay on the highest available point. The original town was located in 1998 by the County Archaeological Unit working with Cambridge University Archaeology Department.

The various attempts to locate the king's attack at Stuntney [Lethbridge in the 1930s] are unconvincing and show only that there were waterborne attacks from various places on the Ouse. Weaponry of eleventh-century type has been found at several places, in the Ouse, in the ditches around Reach and Upware and elsewhere such as Roller's Lode and Dimock's Cote near Wicken, but this shows only that generalised fighting had taken place. It says nothing of William's line of attack. The *Liber Eliensis*, supported by Orderic Vitalis, says that the king advanced against the isle from the castle at Cambridge, set up a base near the River Ouse, possibly at Belsar's Hill near Willingham, and ordered a causeway to be constructed so that he might enter the isle with a cavalry force. William had rightly concluded that any attack using only footsoldiers would fail. As the track from Belsar's Hill neared the River Ouse near Aldreth (a distance of about one mile) the ground would have become softer and boggier, a marsh totally unsuitable for horses, and so a causeway would have been needed there and on the other side of the river. An inspection of the site today reveals a flat plain extending beyond the river on the southern side and several hundred yards to the north, a result of the draining of the Fens in the seventeenth century. In the eleventh century the whole area would have been under water, except for a narrow, winding track. The river itself, then called Aldreth River, flowed west not east as it does today, rising in the watershed west of Stretham. (The flow was reversed sometime in the thirteenth century). Then the ground rises steadily up onto the Isle of Ely towards Linden End in Haddenham. The three vills of Haddenham, Linden End and Hill Row, with Wilburton, were worth £34 a year in 1066 and only £18 when handed back to the abbot, a decline of 55 per cent, evidence of damage from the passage of the Norman army.

The full story of the events of the siege can only be pieced together by attempting to harmonise the conflicting accounts of it given by the two main sources, the *Liber*

Eliensis and the *Gesta Herewardi*. The first is a history of the monastery compiled in the twelfth century by an unknown writer who edited and restyled the version or versions put together, one hesitates to say written, before about 1140. The text ends in about 1174. The siege of Ely is found in Book Two, sections 101 to 111. This presents us with three different versions of the siege. The first, an account of the siege itself, is derived from a text very close to that of the *Gesta Herewardi* but not identical with it, which has been edited to fit the style of the *Liber Eliensis* and which is attributed to the monk Richard of Ely, author according to the text of 'a certain book... of the deeds of Hereward himself' by brother Richard (not the abbot of that name); the second is an account derived from local traditions and using the language of the two Books of Maccabees and borrowings from other writers such as William of Poitiers. These two accounts tend to present the affair as a series of military reverses for King William though they cannot disguise his eventual success. The third, of unknown origin, tells the story very briefly from the Norman point of view, and could derive in part from the reminiscences of the garrison of knights left at Ely after the siege.

The text of the *Gesta Herewardi* is found in the thirteenth-century register of Robert of Swaffham and is a useful confirmation of what the *Liber Eliensis* has to say. By combining this account with the three versions in the *Liber Eliensis* a coherent story can be told, although to do so it is necessary to correct various chronological errors and eliminate some impossibilities. The compiler of the *Liber Eliensis* simply, as he himself admits, put his account together out of many histories ('*e pluribus historiis*') without attempting to reconcile his sources or even realising that he had three separate accounts of the same events. What is more, even the *Gesta Herewardi* repeats some events as if relating a new stage in the fight.

According to all sources the Earl Morcar, accompanied by Bishop Aethelwine of Durham and Siward Barn, had joined Hereward at Ely. No doubt the abbot, Thurstan, and his monks had summoned also the assistance of the thegns, freemen and sokemen of the Isle of Ely, from the 'Two Hundreds that meet at Witchford', to defend the monastery and lands of St Etheldreda (Aethelthryth). The earl would have had his own following of thegns and soke-men, the bishop his lay household, and Siward also those commended to him or under his soke. A number of other leading figures have also been identified among the defend-ers. There was Turchitell, that is Turkill of Harringworth, Northamptonshire. He was the most powerful king's thegn in the Eastern Danelaw, as the *Red Book of Thorney* dem-onstrates. It says there that he deserted his lands after the Conquest because 'he went over to the Danes who were his kinsmen'. He is in the Domesday Book as holding land at Leighton Bromeswold (i.e. Brunneswald), called there Turchil the Dane. He may have been the son of Thorkell the Tall who flourished in Cnut's time. His other main estates were at Sawtry and Connington and after the fall of Ely were given to Earl Waltheof to hold for the king. In total he held 134 hides and 139 carucates in eight shires, a holding of 'baronial' size. Hereward and his men surely received supplies from this man's estates.

Siward of Maldon, in Essex, was a man with wide estates in East Anglia, amounting to some ninety hides and twenty-five carucates in several shires. He is noted to have been *socius Herewardi*, that is his confederate. There were two relatives of Morcar, named as Godric of Corby, termed Morcar's *nepos*, and Tostig of Davenesse (i.e. Daventry), called a *cognatus* (kinsman) of Earl Morcar and to have been named for him at baptism. Another sup-porter was Ordgar the Sheriff of Cambridgeshire. He had retained his office after the Conquest, despite having been a 'man' of King Harold, and was eventually replaced by the

infamous Norman, Picot. Early in William's reign he had
care of the eight and a half hundreds which formed the
Soke or Liberty of Bury St Edmunds, assisted by the thegn
Aelfric Kemp. One of Hereward's other men, in the *Gesta
Herewardi*, is called Alwine son of Ordgar. He forfeited his
lands and office after the fall of Ely. The *Gesta Herewardi*
names a relation (*pronepos*, literally great-grandson!) of
Earl Edwin as 'Turbertinus' who could be the 'Turbatus'
mentioned in a Writ addressed to Lanfranc in 1071 which
grants the archbishop an estate at Freckenham, Suffolk.
This estate was, it says, held by Turbatus and Gotinus 'on
the day when the king crossed the sea'. Before 1066 it
was held of King Harold by a thegn called Orthi who
had perhaps died at Stamford Bridge. These two could
well be his sons and 'Turbertinus' may represent the name
Thorbeorht. All these men would have been accompanied by their own following. The *Gesta Herewardi* gives
a list of some thirty other names of men who cannot be
otherwise identified who are said to be Hereward's men.
Several are described as his relatives, such as Siward Rufus
and Siward Blonde (paternal cousins), the twins Outi and
Duti (nephews) and Winter and Liveret (kinsmen). One
man is named as Rahere, which means the Heron, and
came from Wrokeshambridge. (Wroxham is in Norfolk
Broadland on the River Bure). The rest seem to be card-
board figures named to fill out the background around
Hereward. In all there must have been some 2,000–3,000
combatants on the isle.

King William raised both a land army (*landfyrd*) and a
fleet (*shipfyrd*) which also meant several thousand men and
ordered that the isle be surrounded on all sides, by troops
on the western or landward side and by shipmen (*butsecarls*)
on the eastern or seaward side. The king advanced towards
the isle from the castle at Cambridge and drew near to the
banks of the Ouse, seeking a point from which to launch
an attack.

It was not possible for horsemen to make a crossing without aid, so the king ordered the construction of a causeway (O.E. Brycge) made of wood and stones and faggots of all kinds, with trees and great pieces of timber, all fastened underneath with cowhides inflated with air (or, in the *Liber Eliensis*, sheepskins full of sand). As soon as this was ready the knights rushed on to the structure, eager to seize the gold and silver they thought had been hidden on the isle. But this rather rickety platform collapsed under the weight of men and horses pressing forwards and they were swallowed up in the waters and deep swamp. The compiler of the *Liber Eliensis*, or his source, claims that weapons could still be recovered from the water there in his own times and that many hundreds were said to have perished. Only one man, a knight called Deda, the first to reach the causeway, survived to reach dry land on the other side, where he was captured and taken to Hereward. The knight's story of his time on the isle will be considered below. William, dismayed, retreated, leaving a guard to prevent the defenders breaking out. They are said to have constructed 'ramparts and bulwarks' of earth and peat along the bank of the Ouse to repel attackers. This first attempt took place, according to the *Gesta Herewardi*, at a place identified as Alrehethe which is not exclusively Aldreth (written as Alderethe or Alderede). The obvious meaning of Alrehethe is the *hythe* where the alders grow', which could not refer to the higher land at Stuntney. One clue is that up river from Stuntney lay the Alderbrook, and another is that in the thirteenth century the stretch of river from there to the Granta at Stretham was known as 'Hereward's Reach'. That was possibly opposite Little Thetford where the marsh was narrowed by the Wicken Peninsula, perhaps to the four furlongs of the text. The river below the confluence of the Granta and its tributary streams would have been faster and deeper and that would explain the failure of the first rickety structure.

In the *Liber Eliensis*, the exact location is not named in Section 102 of Book Two. There the river is described as 'swirling', as it would more likely be below the confluence of tributaries than at Aldreth where the river runs through a very flat plain. The *Liber Eliensis* dates these actions to 1069, far too early, but suggesting that this attempt came early in the king's campaign.

The king now considered how he might overcome the isle while at 'Branduna', which is identified as either Brandon near Mildenhall, which suggests that he might have contemplated a waterborne attack, or the royal manor of Brampton near Huntingdon which is somewhat closer to Aldreth. He also ordered the building of a stockade and a ditch or dyke at Reach near Burwell and stationed a garrison there. This is in fact near the Bronze Age earthwork called Devil's Dyke. The Normans would have strengthened the existing works at Reach and erected a palisade. The intention was to confine the Islanders more closely and provide a base for the forces of the king.

Hereward and his men now counter-attacked. The nearby village of Burwell was assaulted, set on fire, and burnt to the ground, although we have no idea of the reason. Perhaps the men of the vill had made supplies available to William's men. The guerrillas then engaged the garrison at Reach which is near one end of the dyke and where Reach Lode overlaps it. A party of Normans, about ten strong, sallied forth to repel the outlaws and drive them back to their boats, but all bar one were slain. At Hereward's intervention one man, named as Richard son of Vicomte Osbert was spared because of his bravery. The main body of Norman troops came up and drove the outlaws back to their boats. Those involved on Hereward's side are said to have included Thurstan called Warden, Siward, Levric, Boter of St Edmunds and Acer the Hard. This local skirmish apparently worried William. In a council of war he asserted that it was impossible to leave these men in his rear at Ely when he needed to move against the Danes and then go to Normandy. (The reference to Danes could be an error for Scots, if the original source merely said Northmen.) After the Ely affair was over he certainly took an army and fleet to Scotland, in 1072, and then intervened in Normandy. The king said that he wished to make peace with the Islanders because 'We cannot prevail against them,' but was dissuaded from doing so by his barons 'because the men of the isle had invaded many of their estates'. This suggests that there had been many more sallies by the defenders than are reported in the sources. Indeed, the *Liber Eliensis* at this point implies that Hereward accepted a truce from the king and that, for a time, he suspended his pillaging operations but that others on the isle, unnamed but possibly meaning Morcar and his supporters, were distrustful of the Normans and kept up their resistance.

Then William grew angry, maintaining that he could not take the isle by storm because it was so well fortified and was protected by the power of God (and presumably his saint, Etheldreda). Ivo Taillebois, a major baron from Lincolnshire, was indignant and instead recommended a renewed assault, with the aid of 'an old woman' (identified elsewhere as a pythoness or witch) who by her spells would crush the defenders' valour and weaken all their defences, and the use of siege towers. The king was apparently persuaded to try it and ordered renewed posting of guards on the isle and a strengthening of the blockade, so combining the practical with the magical. As a result 'almost all the entrances and exits were stopped'. Both sources then return to romantic mode, describing how Hereward, disguised first as a potter selling his wares and then as a fisherman, penetrated the Norman lines and discovered their intentions before being discovered and driven away. He sought refuge at Somersham and returned to the isle by darkness. (This is the sort of feat attributed to heroic leaders, a similar story is told of King Alfred.) It could still be true that he had spies out in the Fens keeping him informed.

William and his men then returned to the vicinity of Aldreth, the text actually reads Alrehede, meaning 'landing place of the alders'. Once there he summoned the aid of all the fishermen in the area to bring their boats to Cotingelade (that is an older Cottenham Lode, as in *Cottyngeslode* in thirteenth-century texts, which means 'watercourse of Cotta's people') loaded with a plentiful supply of wood and other materials with which he intended to build 'mounds and hillocks' from the top of which an attack could be launched. His soldiers, both footmen and knights, were in all likelihood based in a camp at Belsar's Hill (from Belasis, or 'beautiful seat'), a former Iron Age fort used also by the Romans near Willingham, which would have served as a basis for a fortified encampment, needing only a stockade. This *castellum* controlled the existing narrow causeway, unusable by horsemen, leading to the river crossing at Aldreth.

He then built four circular siege towers on which he placed 'engines' (or in the *Liber Eliensis*, *ballistae*, that is, catapults). These would have protected the peasantry labouring to widen and strengthen the track to make it usable by horses. The men of the isle are again said to have built ramparts for their defence. 'For certain of them had made out of the accumulated turf some defensive works beyond the walls on the bank of the aforesaid river.' This must surely refer to improvised defences on the river bank, certainly at Aldreth and probably also along the Ouse at Ely. Waterborne attacks would have been launched from lower down, below Ely, to draw the defenders' attention away from Aldreth. From the other side of the river, both at Aldreth and at Ely, William bombarded the defences. The catapults were used to soften up the enemy, and then, after eight days, the witch was brought along and placed on top of one of the towers. She now began to curse the defenders, 'denouncing destruction and uttering charms' (and, it is said, displaying her naked buttocks, a tale paralleled by that of an Englishman at Exeter who insulted the Normans by exposing his genitals and farting). The only effect was to provoke the defenders, who sallied forth through the fen and set fire to the reeds and briars surrounding the Norman position (using oil and pitch to make sure the damp sedge burned well) and set alight the king's wooden towers. Fire was Hereward's favourite weapon, used also at Peterborough and Burwell. The Normans were driven back by the flames and dense smoke, leaving the witch hysterical with fear and shrieking imprecations, stranded on her tower. Overcome by the smoke, she fell head first and broke her neck. William was again left to contemplate the results of his poor planning.

The account in both texts then loses all sense of chronology and confuses the siege of Ely with the Revolt of the Earls (of East Anglia and Hereford) which occurred in 1075. The writer of this section, his head full of the siege of Troy, wanted to make the siege of Ely last seven years, from 1069 to 1075 inclusive. He actually mentions the Aeneid of Virgil and the Thebaid. This is again romance not history. In fact King William, aware that force had not worked, now resorted to guile. Making sure that the announcement reached the monks on the isle, he issued a decree to divide among his more eminent followers the lands of the Church; the monks heard of this and the abbot, returning from 'Angerhale' (a hamlet of Bottisham, Cambridgeshire) where he had hidden the Ely treasure and ornaments, sued for peace, asking of William that he restore to them all the lands of the Church freely and honourably.

The king agreed. This was to be done in secret, concealing it from Hereward. It was then arranged that the king should come to the isle while Hereward was absent with a foraging party. Hereward was forewarned of these arrangements by a monk, Alwine son of Ordgar, who intercepted Hereward when he was planning to burn down the church and the town (presumably to render them of no use to the Normans) and urged him to flee because the king and his army were already at Witchford. If this decree was issued and believed by the monks, then they were deceived. The king had already assured his followers that they would have permanent possession of their fiefs free from any obligation to pay customary dues to the abbey.

Orderic Vitalis has his own highly coloured account. As he tells it, the king was persuaded by his barons to deceive the rebels by offering to accept their submission, as he had that of several others on previous occasions. Morcar, in particular, was told that if he were to return to the king he would be received in peace as a faithful or loyal friend. As Orderic puts it, 'crafty messengers' proposed 'treacherous terms' so that Morcar, deceived, surrendered.

What seems to have happened is this. Knowing that Abbot Thurstan and the monks, and therefore their men, would not oppose him, and warned by Thurstan of Hereward's absence, William had first constructed a guardhouse at Aldreth (a *castello*) and then set about building a bridge over the Ouse and strengthening existing stretches of causeway through the swamp, using small boats not only to bring up his supplies, but to form a pontoon bridge at Aldreth. The boats were tied together and a road of staves and hurdles laid on top of them, permitting the cavalry to pass over. Shallow or waterlogged areas would have been filled in with rocks and stones to form a track. The landing was given covering fire by the catapults (*ballistae*) and by men adept at throwing 'darts', that is, javelins.

It was still a very risky venture. The men, in their heavy armour, were deterred by the difficulties presented by the need to cross the marsh against the fire of enemy arrows and by the obstacle presented by the marsh itself, 'a whirlpool of solid matter loosened by streams and rivers'. These waters ran in 'treacherous beds' in which deep cracks appeared unexpectedly as the mud readily split open, and heavy rain and hail assailed the knights. The marsh was of 'horrific appearance and of infinite depth, festering all around to the deepest parts of its hollow bed'. The causeway is described as narrow and winding (which fits the track from Belsar's Hill to Aldreth) and in need of strengthening if it was to be used by cavalry. In the course of their advance the knights found themselves, in places, passing over the bodies of dead horses, killed in the earlier struggle, as if over a bridge. They were attacked as they advanced by the defenders and some were killed. Then, we are told, 'The king rapidly led his army across by a weak and wobbly bridge made on little boats with poles and wicker hurdles'.

Having thus crossed the Aldreth Ouse, the soldiery met even more marsh with standing waters and fast flowing streams. But they overran and demolished the siege works, constructed by the defenders out of blocks of peat, from which they had thrown stones and other missiles. While the attack via the causeway and its pontoon bridge was being made, the king used his fleet to seize control of the rivers around Ely to prevent access to the coast for anyone seeking to escape.

The attacking force consisted of all the French knights with the king. As the *Liber Eliensis* says, 'A thousand French cavalry, mailed and helmeted, who had crossed over (the river) were attacking three thousands of the pirates and many more English soldiers gathered from the inland regions called by the common people, the isle.' Geoffrey Gaimar in his account speaks not only of knights but of sergeants and shipmen and also of 'privateers', that is, mercenary troops. This attack was unexpected and the *Liber Eliensis* claims 'The king, however, brought the army safe right up to the waters of Ely, much closer than the opinion of anybody had predicted... Then the loud voice of victory most quickly drove the enemies from the isle.'

The attack had been made possible by what the *Liber Eliensis* calls 'an amazing feat of engineering' as William brought up little boats carrying the 'siege-engines' which were erected on them and from which he was able to bombard the defenders so heavily that 'the unstable ground shook'. Even after crossing the river, the men had to struggle uphill towards Haddenham across more pools of water, scarcely able to make their way to solid ground because of 'pitfalls and eddies of mud'.

Passing Haddenham, William was confronted by more marsh where the obvious route from Aldreth to Ely runs via the flint causeways linking the fen islands, which would naturally bring King William to Witchford by skirting around the area known today as Grunty Fen, still well below sea level. He is said to have followed 'the crooked fen paths on a most difficult marsh' and so was able to surround the enemy in an ambush.

That the fighting occurred in this area is perhaps confirmed by the fall in values of the manors, as recorded in Domesday Book, of 40 per cent, which affected all the villages between Aldreth and Ely. Cottenham, Impington, Willingham, Sutton and Haddenham were affected, as well as Witcham, Witchford and Wilburton, Little Downham and Little Thetford. Having thus won his way onto the island, William swiftly drove the enemy from it, and accepted the surrender of the magnates who had been led to expect fair treatment. But notably not that of Hereward's band which slipped away via the Ouse and the Wellstream near Upwell where 'he withdrew into a great sea called Wide beside Welle, a great and spacious body of water with shores having ready escape routes'. William himself paid a quick visit to the church at Ely, though he dared not approach St Etheldreda's shrine too closely, and returned to Witchford (described as being 'at a short distance from Ely on the road to Aldreth'). There he interviewed Abbot Thurstan, accepted his submission, though fining him heavily, and guaranteed the Church the full possession of its lands. The monks had already given the king 700 marks, but now had to find another 300 for not welcoming the king when he visited their church. Thurstan is reported to have met the king again a little later at Warwick and to have been given a charter confirming Ely's possession of its estates. The language of that charter is used in the *Liber Eliensis* in discussing the terms on which Thurstan agreed to surrender the isle.

One consequence for the abbey was that the abbot was required by order of the king to retain in the hall of the monastery a number of soldiers (probably knights are meant) for protection, that is a *praesidium* or garrison located within the monks' enclosure, and to provide them with a stipend and daily ration of food. It is this that has created the impression that William built a castle at Ely; the sources say only that he built one at Wisbech. No castle is mentioned for Ely until the reign of Henry I at which time the abbey was permitted, at a price, to perform its service of castle guard at Ely and not, as previously, at Norwich. In Stephen's reign the rebel Bishop Nigel built a fort of lime and stone (which St Etheldreda repeatedly caused to fall down) and then one of timber and 'walled in the round hill called the keep'. Later references to a *Castelbrigge* and *Castelhythe* imply merely that there was both a bridge and a hythe or landing stage reserved for the use of the castle garrison, probably protected by a guardhouse.

In the end any promises made by William were broken. The nobles involved were all, contrary to what they had been led to expect, imprisoned, that is Morcar, Aethelwine and Siward Barn. Morcar was placed in the custody of Roger Beaumont and remained a prisoner until the end of the reign. William, on his deathbed, released Morcar along with other captives, but William Rufus promptly re-arrested him and he died in captivity. Siward Barn too was imprisoned. He is also said to have been released and exiled. One possibility is that he ended up as a member of the Varangian Guard at Byzantium. Bishop Aethelwine was confined to a monastery and died a few months later. The leaders of the second rank were most cruelly dealt with; although the principals were imprisoned, the others were deprived of hands, eyes or feet. The large number of the common people were released unpunished. As for Hereward, he and his men slipped away to the forest called 'Brunneswald' and out of history into romance. Such facts as can be gleaned about his eventual fate are considered further in a discussion of his career and identity.

What of King William's famous 'causeway'? The *Chronicles* report that he built a causeway, two miles long in one version (Florence), and so came on to the isle. It is the *Liber Eliensis* and the *Gesta Herewardi*, knowing rather more about the terrain perhaps, which insist on a pontoon bridge. Such a structure would certainly have been needed to cross the Ouse, while a causeway was not so much built from scratch as widened and strengthened to provide cavalry access. Matthew Paris, an admittedly late source, talks about 'roads of great length' constructed in the swamps to render 'those great deeps passable by men and animals' and adds that William then built a castle, not at Ely but at Wisbech. Aldreth was, in the eleventh century, located on the 'Aldreth River', which flowed west into the Old Ouse which then flowed north from Earith to Upwell (and from there into the Well Creek at Outwell). Environmental changes in the thirteenth century caused the formation of the Old West River which flowed in the opposite direction to Stretham, to join the Cam.

It is also clear that there were waterborne attacks from the eastern side, from Brandon on the Little Ouse and from Reach on the Cam. The *Peterborough Chronicle* (E) says he surrounded the district 'building a causeway as he advanced deeper into the Fens, while a naval force remained to seaward.' Florence agrees that sailors were used to blockade the eastern side. Modern military historians such as Matthew Bennett (Sandhurst) maintain that the attack was an amphibious assault by the fleet combined with a landward attack and that William constructed not one but several causeways. That the crossing at Aldreth made use of a pontoon bridge, as reported by the *Liber Eliensis*, is confirmed by the report in the *Gesta Stephani*. When King Stephen came to Ely to drive out the rebel bishop, Nigel, he imitated the Conqueror by building a bridge of boats at Aldreth (that is 'a floating bridge' *Gesta Stephani* 62) where he captured the '*castellulum*' or small castle there, that is the guard house and palisade built to defend the entry to the isle. Perhaps that was what later writers like Matthew Paris meant when they spoke of the existence of a wooden castle in the Fens called 'Hereward's Castle'. Stephen was aided by one of the monks who betrayed the defenders and was later made Abbot of Ramsey. A final piece of evidence lies in the collected writs of the Conqueror, No. 155 in the *Regesta Regum*, addressed to Archbishop Lanfranc, the Count of Mortain and Bishop Geoffrey of Coutances, in 1082. It commands an enquiry into the lands of Ely Abbey, ordering them to be restored to the monks as they were held in King Edward's day. But remarkably it ends 'Lastly, those men are to maintain the causeway at Ely who by the king's command have done so hitherto'.

The famous causeway was carefully maintained throughout the Conqueror's reign and thereafter cheerfully neglected.

8

The Hereward of History

The history of the resistance to the Norman Conquest, in which unknown thousands of thegns took part, is focused in literature almost entirely on one man: Hereward, hero of the defence of Ely. It was probably his pre-emptive strike against Peterborough that ensured that he rather than anyone else was remembered, a question of luck, perhaps, rather than good judgement, which was enhanced when he remained at Ely after the Danes left. In addition to that, he was a local man. Later the Wakes were to use his legend to give colour to a rather spurious pedigree.

Who exactly was this man Hereward? Hereward the Exile or Hereward the Outlaw certainly, but Hereward the Wake, never. That description was applied to him, probably some time in the late twelfth century, by the family of Wake, descendants of Geoffrey Wac or Wake and his son Hugh who had married Emma, daughter of a minor baron called Baldwin fitzGilbert and by so doing acquired Baldwin's estates and manor of Bourne in Lincolnshire. The Wacs or Wakes now owned several pieces of land once owned by or associated with Hereward, including Bourne itself. The Wakes were not content merely to claim descent from Hereward, and such a claim is not an impossible one, but also that he himself was called 'le Wake' which is quite absurd. No early source uses the phrase. Matthew Paris writing in the early thirteenth century, tells us that there was a '*castrum*', which can mean either castle or camp, made of wood in the Fens in his own time and still referred to as the castle of Hereward (*castellum Herewardi*) but does not use the term 'Wake'. Other sources do call him 'le Wake' including the *History of Crowland*, allegedly by Ingulf, the Abbot of Crowland at the end of the eleventh century, (but actually a fourteenth-century work of what we might call 'faction', a mixture of fact and fiction, by an unknown monk of Crowland, usually referred to as the *Pseudo-Ingulf*) and then the so-called *Chronicle of Abbot John of Peterborough*, published and printed by Joseph Sparke in 1723 in *Historiae Anglicanae Scriptores Varii* and perhaps more accurately termed the *Annales Burgo-Spaldenses*. This again was the work of an anonymous monk of fourteenth-century Peterborough. It consists of miscellaneous 'annals' written to mark the passing years.

TRADITIONAL ACCOUNTS

Both the *Gesta Herewardi* and *Pseudo-Ingulf* provide details of Hereward's alleged parentage and so does the claim put forward for Edmund de Holand, Earl of Kent in 1407 alleging his descent from Hereward through the Wake family (Cott.Chart.xiii.9) in the female line, naming Hereward's daughter as Turfrida like her mother. This gives his father's name, as do other late sources, as Leofric and alleges that this is Leofric, Earl of Mercia (calling him Earl of Chester). The other, earlier, sources are content to call him 'Leofric of Bourne'.

The son of Earl Leofric is well known. He was Aelfgar, Earl of East Anglia while his father lived and Earl of Mercia after him. He was twice exiled or outlawed by King Edward the Confessor, allegedly for treason but probably for objecting to the advancement of the sons of Godwin, and was last heard of in 1062. He had three sons, Burgheard, who died in 1061 at Rheims, Edwin, who became Earl of Mercia after his father, and Morcar, Earl of Northumbria after 1065, and incidentally said by Domesday Book to have held land in Bourne before the Conquest. There is no room for a brother to Aelfgar or a fourth son not mentioned by the Chroniclers. We can dismiss a putative descent of Hereward from the great earl, while recognising that the career of Earl Aelfgar provides the outlines of the story later applied to Hereward of outlawry and exile.

The other sources also try to provide Hereward with an earl in his ancestry, no doubt because heroes need noble ancestors. Unfortunately, the two accounts given contradict each other and are riddled with errors. First up is the *Gesta Herewardi,* which states that his father was Leofric of Bourne son of 'Earl Radulf surnamed Scabre', which looks like a corruption of 'Earl Ralph surnamed Staller' (Stalre). More credibly, Hereward's mother is said to have been Aediva, great-great-granddaughter of a Duke Oslac who flourished *c.*962 in the service of Edgar, King of Mercia, Northumbria and Wessex. But we know who the son of Ralph the Staller was, Ralph Guader or of Gael (that is 'the Breton') also Earl of East Anglia like his father. There is no record of a son called Leofric, which is an English name, and the Staller was probably half Breton, so an English name for a son would be highly unlikely.

The alternative, and contradictory, version is that of the *Pseudo-Ingulf*. It looks like a development from an account similar to but not identical with the *Gesta Herewardi*. In *Ingulf* a knight called Leofric, Lord of 'Brunne', that is Bourne, is a relative (not son) of 'Radin, Earl of Hertford who married Goda, sister of King Edward, and who is buried at Peterborough' (a variant reading gives 'Ralph'). This is plainly meant to be Earl Ralph of Mantes, Earl of Hereford and nephew of King Edward (writing Hertford for Hereford) but he was the son of Edward's sister Goda, not married to her. Leofric is again the husband of Aediva but she is said to be the niece of Duke Oslac 'the contemporary of the late King Edgar'. This is chronologically impossible; King Edgar died in 975 and Oslac is last mentioned in 966!

All of these accounts must be rejected as attempts to provide Hereward with a noble lineage befitting so great a hero. Elsewhere in the sources, not only the partially legendary accounts but in the major *Chronicles* also, he is presented as the associate of English and Danish nobles. He raids Peterborough in the company of Danes led by the sons of Swein Estrithson, King of Denmark, and the king's brother Bjorn, then he defends Ely alongside Earl Morcar and other leading English nobles such as Siward Barn, Siward of Maldon and Turchil of Harringworth. His activities at Peterborough and Ely have been considered in earlier chapters. They are based on the *Chronicle of Hugh Candidus* and on the *Old English* or *Anglo-Saxon Chronicle*, both of which used an earlier account of Hereward's activities than the accounts in the *Gesta Herewardi* and *Liber Eliensis* and now lost. The *Chronicle* version (D) in particular is written in an almost contemporary hand and shows local knowledge of the Ely campaign.

THE KNOWN BACKGROUND

That Hereward was a genuine leader of the English
Resistance is plain from his activities, those of a guerrilla
leader and probably one of the *silvatici*. They are given in the
Peterborough version (E) of the *Anglo-Saxon Chronicle* and
the writings of Hugh Candidus, monk of Peterborough.
But clues to his origins are found in the pages of Domesday
Book, which contain the earliest known references to him.
He is found to have held various small amounts of land
in several places scattered around but not in Bourne in
Lincolnshire, as might be expected from a thegn's son who
had not yet inherited his father's lands. We are told that
he held twelve bovates (that is one and a half carucates) at
Witham-on-the-Hill, Manthorpe, Toft and Lund, which
in 1086 were held by 'Asuert' (that is, Asford or Asfrothr)
the 'man' of Abbot Turold of Peterborough. A berewick
or detached portion of this manor lay in Barholme and
Stow where Asford held another carucate. Stow itself was
rated at four bovates. In Laughton, Hereward, in conjunction with a certain Toli, held four bovates of land worth
forty shillings. A berewick of Laughton in Aslackby and
Avethorpe was rated at six bovates. The carucate was the
Danelaw equivalent of the hide, and subdivided into eight
bovates, while the hide was subdivided into four virgates.
By 1066 both of these were units of account for the raising
of the *geld* or land tax and represented a sort of rateable
value.

In the section at the end of the account for Lincolnshire,
called the '*Clamores*' or Complaints, we are told that the
Wapentake (the equivalent in the Danelaw of the hundred
court) maintained that Hereward did not actually own the
land in Barholme 'on the day he fled'. As the information
sought by the commissioners was concerned with the state
of affairs before the Conquest, that is, 'in the time of King
Edward', this mention of Hereward's flight must refer to

his outlawry as related in the *Gesta Herewardi*. But this is not all. The Wapentake also comments on Land of St Guthlac, that is Crowland Abbey, held in 1086 by Ogier the Breton. This is worth quoting in full.

> Land of St Guthlac which Ogier holds in Rippingale; they say that it was of the demesne farm of the monks and that Abbot Ulfcytel commended it to the farm of Hereward as it might be agreed between them each year, but the abbot took it back before Hereward fled the country as he had not kept the agreement.

Thus Hereward is said to have made an agreement with the abbot to lease Rippingale, which was part of the abbey's home farm, for a rental or set amount of service and/or money to be agreed between them each year, but Hereward had lost the land because he did not keep his side of the bargain. This was apparently immediately before his exile and as Ulfcytel became abbot in 1062, this suggests that Hereward was outlawed in 1063. The Abbot Ulfcytel remained in office until deposed by a synod in 1085 'because he was English born and vile to the Normans' says Orderic Vitalis. Other entries reveal how much land was involved. The abbey had three carucates in Rippingale, of which Ogier had the use, which was intended 'for the monks' supplies'. Ogier also had two carucates in Ringstone and Rippingale. What is more, Ogier held land in Bourne, which perhaps explains the idea that Hereward, who was Ogier's predecessor elsewhere, also held land there.

Hereward's lands, including what he had lost or never fully acquired, amount to about nine carucates, a reasonable amount for a young man who had not yet been given an estate by his father. The agreement with the abbot suggests that he had been offered the chance of becoming the abbey's protector or advocate, which implies that he was potentially more than a median or middle-ranking thegn.

His failure to keep to the agreement seems to confirm the suggestion in the *Gesta Herewardi* that he was a head-strong young man. We do not know exactly why he was exiled, but the *Gesta Herewardi* says that he was accused of sedition. Certainly he was, in this respect, in some quite distinguished company. Earl Aelfgar of Mercia had been twice exiled for political reasons, which probably meant opposing the aims and plans of the Godwinson clan. The whole of the family of Godwin, Earl of Wessex, had been exiled in 1051, to both Ireland and Flanders, after a quarrel with King Edward, and Earl Godwin's son Swein had first abandoned his earldom then fled abroad for a time after being accused of the rape of the Abbess of Leominster, or perhaps because he was not then allowed to marry her; and then, after being permitted to return, was outlawed and declared 'nithing', a man without honour, because he murdered his cousin Beorn. He died in exile while returning from a pilgrimage to Jerusalem. Even Osgod Clapa, a former associate of Cnut the Great, was exiled, to Flanders, probably because he was seen as a threat to the king as he sent his men to wreak havoc along the Essex coast whilst he was himself detained in Flanders. This use of outlawry suggests that the usual reason for exiling a man was that he represented a political threat. Earl Tostig was exiled in 1065 after Northumbria rebelled against him. Nothing is known of the fate of Earl Aelfgar of Mercia: the *Chronicles* simply cease to mention him after 1062. Perhaps he rebelled against Edward once too often and died as a result. If so, Hereward might have been involved in such an affair or some other matter that the records do not mention. There is nothing to help us decide, but that he was exiled is certain. One of the consequences of outlawry, a penalty introduced by Cnut the Great, and which put a man beyond the protection of the law, was that the book-land (land granted by charter or 'book') of an outlawed thegn was forfeited into the hands of the king (II Cnut

13, par.1) without regard to the question of whose man he was, but loanland returned to the lord who had title to it. Hereward's Rippingale land was loanland and returned to the abbot. Bookland was land over which a man had sake and soke and free disposal. The lands Hereward is said to have held before 1066 all seem to be loanland and by 1086 were held by Peterborough or Crowland Abbeys (or by Norman lords under the abbots). It could be that his bookland had already returned to the king, in which case it is an untraceable part of royal lands in Lincolnshire. Many of his local supporters would have been in the same position. An outlawed thegn could only be granted peace by the king in person.

THE REAL HEREWARD?

Is it possible to say anything more about his family origins? Perhaps so. There is one clue, largely overlooked so far. Two sources, both very late and of uncertain reliability, state quite simply that Abbot Brand of Peterborough was his uncle. The first reference comes from that same *Pseudo-Ingulf* which made such a hash of its account of his parentage. This account says that Hereward desired to be made a knight, to put himself on even terms with his Norman opponents, and that he went to Abbot Brand 'who was his uncle' to seek knighthood. The story is obviously derived from the same tale given in the *Gesta Herewardi*, from which 'Ingulf' appears to be borrowing, but the reference to Brand as Hereward's uncle is not in the *Gesta Herewardi*. If that were all, then it could be assumed that this was a bit of *Pseudo-Ingulf*'s embroidery. But the same information, in a most interesting form, is provided by the *Annales Burgo-Spaldenses*, a fourteenth-century source most easily accessible in the footnotes to W.T. Mellow's edition of the *Peterborough Chronicle* of Hugh Candidus. (This is the earliest source to use the phrase 'Hereward le

Wake' and indicates that it had become usual to refer to Hereward in this way, possibly because of the claims of the Wake family to be descended from him.) The notice in question reads:

> AD 1069. There died Brand Abbot of Peterborough, paternal uncle (patruus) of the said Hereward le Wake, to whom by the King's choice there succeeded Turold.

The text says something about Abbot Brand rather than about Hereward; he is that Brand who was paternal uncle to 'Hereward le Wake' and who was succeeded by Turold. The second part of the statement, and the date of his death, are both accurate. Several other entries in these *Annales* concern Hereward or Turold or both, mainly derived from the *Gesta Herewardi* or something very like it. Those modern historians who mention the relationship, such as D.C. Douglas, appear to accept it without question and it is not the sort of detail which could be easily invented, especially the use of '*patruus*', which is very specific in its meaning. This kind of connection is usually expressed the other way round, as when we are told by Orderic Vitalis, that Eadric the Wild was '*nepos*' to Eadric Streona, literally nephew but used of several different relationships from son to grandson, cousin, nephew or great-nephew.

If Abbot Brand was the paternal uncle of Hereward it follows that Hereward's father is to be found among the brothers of the abbot. Brand had four brothers, Aschil, Siric, Siworth and Godric. We also know that their father was called Toki. Three of the brothers can be discounted as Hereward's father. Taking them in reverse order, Godric, the youngest, was a monk at Peterborough. In 1098 he was chosen by the monks to replace Abbot Turold. Unfortunately, as William Rufus was still king, the monks had found themselves obliged to pay him a consider-able sum of money for permission to elect Godric. After

the accession of Henry I and the return of Archbishop
Anselm, Godric was removed from office, rather unfairly,
on the charge of simony because of the payment to
Rufus. Possibly he was really rejected, like Abbot Ulfcytel,
because he was English. He was obviously too young to
be Hereward's father. Of the other two, Siric and Siworth,
little is known, but an entry in Domesday Book sheds
some light. The entries for North and South Muskham
in Nottinghamshire record that on the land of Geoffrey
Alselin, the Norman successor in all his lands of a certain
Toki of Lincoln, land was held of him by 'Siward' (i.e.;
Siworth/Sigvatr) in North Muskham, and on more of his
land in South Muskham, land was held of him by 'Seric'
(i.e. Siric). In addition, at West Keal, Lincolnshire, 'Siric the
Thegn' still held twelve bovates of land. This man also had
three bovates at Theddlethorpe and more at Sutton in the
Marsh. This does look like the brothers of Brand surviving
until 1086. But if so, then they are also too young for either
of them to be Hereward's father.

That leaves 'Aschil the King's thegn'. This is Aschil (also
written variously as Askill or Eskill, representing a hypo-
coristic contraction of the name Asketill) who is described
as the son of Toki in the *Black Book of Peterborough* (the
collection of the abbey's charters and other documents).
He held an estate at Manton on lease from his brother
'Brand the monk'; and in the Domesday Clamores for
the West Riding of Lincolnshire he is said to have held
lands from King Edward 'and later' (that is under Harold)
at Scotter, Scotton and Raventhorpe '*in propria libertate*',
literally 'in his own free possession', freely and with soke
and sake. These lands are found in Domesday Book as
possessions of Peterborough Abbey because Abbot Brand
had arranged to hold all of them in order to keep them
out of the hands of Norman lords. There were six carucates
at Scotton, eight carucates at Scotter (with another three
at Scotterthorpe, a berewick or detached portion of the

manor) and two carucates at Raventhorpe. Aschil also held six carucates at Walcote-on-Trent (described as 'near the River Humber') and finally one carucate in Barholme and Stow. That is a total of some twenty-six carucates (the Danelaw equivalent of Hides). The Wapentake (or shire court of the Danelaw) reports that Aschil was a King's thegn. For comparison, King's thegns in Cambridgeshire are recorded as holding as follows; Sigar twenty-nine hides, Aelmer twenty hides, Ordmer nineteen hides. Other lands in Lincolnshire are attributed to someone called Aschil, but this is not the same man as Toki's son as he has three different brothers.

There is evidence that land was transferred to the Abbey. A charter, allegedly issued by King Edward, states that 'Aschil, King Edward's thegn' gave land at Walcote *'iuxta fluvium Humbrae'* to Abbot Leofric and Peterborough Abbey when he was about to go to Rome on pilgrimage so that the abbey would have the land after his death and those of his brothers Siric and Siworth. Another charter, also allegedly from King Edward, confirms the agreement between Brand and his family to lease estates to his brother 'Aschil' in Scotton, Scotter and Manton for a yearly rental, with 'Thorpe' in exchange for Manton. The second charter records that Brand obtained three estates for Aschil; one, Scotton, he bought himself, one, Manton, given by his father Toki and a third, Scotter, by his brother Siric. The charters are viewed with some suspicion as possible forgeries but the transactions in them are accepted as genuine because they are essentially confirmed by Hugh Candidus in his *History of the Abbey*. He lists the lands in question and says of them 'This is what Brand the monk (and afterwards abbot) of Peterborough and Aschil and Siric and Siworth his brothers gave to God and St Peter and the brothers of Burgh'. The charters were probably modelled on genuine exemplars and concocted after the Conquest to convince King William that Peterborough rightfully owned these lands. If so, they were successful because a Writ (Regesta I No. 8) confirms Abbot Brand's lands in their entirety, that is 'the lands that his brothers or kinsmen held hereditarily and freely under King Edward', and the abbey retained these lands thereafter.

That Aschil was Hereward's father would also seem to be confirmed by his holding land in Barholme and Stow, since it is concerning this estate that the Wapentake asserted that Hereward did not have it on the day he fled. His Norman successor elsewhere, Asfort, or Asfrothr, the 'man' of Abbot Turold, would certainly have tried to claim this land as part of Hereward's holding, but the Wapentake had already given evidence that it belonged to Aschil. In Henry I's time a charter given at Oxford in 1114 restoring lands to Peterborough Abbey 'as when Turold was alive and dead' with the service of certain knights, includes Asford of Witham-on-the Hill among them. The Norman must have had some reason for thinking that it had been Hereward's land, as heir of Aschil perhaps. Only Aschil held land in the vicinity of Bourne, close to most of the other lands held by Hereward, the other brothers held land in northern Lincolnshire. One more point about Aschil's Lincolnshire lands is made in a writ of William Rufus (Regesta I 409) dated to 1093-98 and addressed to Robert, Bishop of Lincoln and Osbern the sheriff. It grants to Peterborough Abbey the lands of Ivo Taillebois 'that he held of the monks and restored in his lifetime as in the chirograph between Ivo and (Abbot) Turold'. These included the lands of Aschil at Scotter and Walcot among lands previously seized by Ivo.

Aschil may have been much more important and much wealthier than appears from the description of his lands given so far. He is the 'Aschill Tokesune' witnessing the charter by which King Edward confirmed the gift of an estate at Fiskerton to Peterborough in 1060 and he is Askyl filius Toke in Walter of Whittlesey's additions to the *Chronicle of Hugh Candidus*. Walter gives a long list of lands, about a dozen, belonging to the abbey, Walcote, Muskham and Scotter among them, and then says 'This is what Brand, monk and afterwards abbot, and Aschil and Siric and Siworth, brothers, gave to God and St Peter and the brothers of Burgh.' Aschil seems to have held land in other shires. In Bedfordshire a king's thegn called 'Eskill' held a total of twelve different estates (for example Stotfold, later held by Azelina, widow of Ralph Taillebois) and another five were held by men commended to him. He was predecessor in Bedfordshire to Ralph Taillebois. He appears again in Huntingdonshire at Covington and Winwick, another eleven hides, held as elsewhere with sake and soke. It seems unlikely that there were two East Midlands king's thegns called Aschil and this lends prob-ability to the suggestion that he was the wealthy king's thegn known as Aschil 'of Ware'. He is identified as the same man as the Aschil at Covington who also held land at Wickham in Hertfordshire and a berewick at Stotfold which was an outlier of the manor of Ware. This manor of Ware was rated at twenty-four hides and was worth £50 a year and was clearly his chief seat. He had nine hides in Northamptonshire, and is found also in Huntingdonshire, Leicestershire and Essex. The name has differing forms of the same personal name, Eskil is the Danish spelling and Aschill is Norse. In the charter mentioned earlier his name is spelt 'Askytelo'.

There is a likely identity for Aschil's father, Toki. The most prominent holder of that name in Lincolnshire, pos-sibly the only man so named, was the burgess, as we may term him, Toki of Lincoln, also called Toki son of Outi (or Auti). He was one of those listed as having 'sake and soke and toll and team' in Lincolnshire, that is, valuable rights of jurisdiction and control over markets, and after the Conquest almost all of his property passed to the Norman Geoffrey Alselin. He is listed in Domesday in the

company of prominent men like Siward Barn and
Maerleswein. Toki had his chief residence, his hall, in
Lincoln, where he owned large amounts of property. He
owned thirty 'messuages', that is houses with land attached
and two and a half churches, which became Geoffrey's
property, and had another thirty messuages over which
he had letting rights and received one silver penny annually. Thirty of Toki's messuages were seized, not entirely
lawfully, by Bishop Remigius when he moved his see
from Dorchester to Lincoln, and were used as the site
of Lincoln Cathedral. He held land in several counties
and this suggests that he is an example of a merchant
who had become wealthy and so 'thegnrightworthy' and
whose equally wealthy son became a king's thegn. If Aschil
was Hereward's father and Toki his grandfather, then he
certainly was, as Geoffrey Gaimar puts it, 'one of the first
in the land' and it would explain the insistence of other
writers that he had noble ancestry. King's thegns were men
with a close relationship, by service, to the king, among
those with 'seat and special duty in the king's hall'. As the
document 'Of People's Ranks and Laws' has it:

> And if a thegn throve, so that he served the king, and on his
> summons rode among his household; if he then had a thegn
> who him followed… he might thenceforth with his 'foreoath'
> his lord represent at various needs.

It is thought that there were some 200 king's thegns, ranking below the earls but above thegns of middle rank, and
holding estates that the Normans would have regarded as
of baronial extent. The document of the twelfth century
called the 'Leis Willelme', a compendium of Anglo-Norman
custom, equates a king's thegn with the rank of baron, as
it equates earl to count. With the earls the king's thegns
formed the upper ranks of the English aristocracy. There
were two sorts of king's thegns, 'he who has his soke' and

he who has 'a closer relationship with the king'. As both Aschil and Brand were able to obtain charters from King Edward, the thegn would seem to belong to the second and higher category. King's thegns owed 'heriot' to the king, that is, on their death their arms and armour and a sum of money returned to the king. This reveals the kind of 'war gear' they were expected to have; four horses, lances and shields, one helmet and tunic (mailed hauberk) and one sword, with fifty mancuses of gold (or £6 5s). Such men attended the king periodically at Court, holding office there by rotation, and kept the king in touch with the shires. They could be used for occasional business in which the king had a personal interest and kings regarded the maintenance of their dignity as necessary for the honour of the crown. Aschil or Asketil the king's thegn is the best nominee as the father of Hereward.

If this is accepted, and that Toki of Lincoln was the head of the family in Edward's reign, other relatives appear. A certain Haelfdan, who is listed in the Lincolnshire Domesday as 'Aldene', and was said to be a kinsman of Abbot Brand, had all his land, over fifteen carucates, including some at Dunsby, near Bourne, taken from him and given to Bishop Remigius of Lincoln before 1069 (when Brand died) so the abbot leased to him an estate at Dunsby given to the abbey by Elfgar of Dunsby. In 1086 Remigius successfully claimed that this land had not belonged to the abbey in King Edward's time. According to the *Descriptio Terrarum* of Peterborough Abbey (dated to 1071-86) Barholme, at four carucates, was sokeland belonging to 'Haldene' and was under the soke (or jurisdiction) of Witham. Haelfdan was brother of Ulf Topeson whose lands went, like those of Toki, to Geoffrey Alselin. Domesday Book calls him 'Halfdene Tope', that is Topesune. He also is described as kin to Brand. Ulf Topesune lost his land at around the same time or after Hereward's rising. This Ulf had given Manthorpe and Carlton to the abbey. In 1066 or 1067 he

witnesses the confirmation of the abbey's lands to Abbot
Brand by King William (Writ No. 8 in Regesta) alongside dignitaries like Ealdred, Maerleswein and William
fitzOsbern. There is a will of this Ulf, and his wife Madselin,
made before their pilgrimage to Jerusalem, leaving land at
Carlton Scroop to Peterborough and Bytham to Crowland
and Sempringham to Ramsey Abbey. Land was to be sold
at Lavington 'for its full price' to Archbishop Ealdred
(who showed the king's seal to the Wapentake in 1086 and
recovered the land from a certain Hibold). If Ealdred died
first, Brand was to be given the land. Ulf also bequeathed
Manthorpe 'in Witham-on-the-Hill' to Brand and other
lesser bequests were also made as well as dispositions for
prayers for their souls should they die. Claxby was given
by Ulf to Haelfdan his brother. He was surely one of the
'good men' who interceded with King William on Brand's
behalf in 1066. It looks very likely that Toki and Tope were
brothers. It is clear that Hereward was very well connected
indeed before 1066.

9

Hereward in Exile

Earlier chapters have dealt with Hereward's activities at Peterborough and Ely, and consideration is now given to what is known of his career while in exile. The exiling of Hereward had occurred probably in 1063. Domesday Book twice records the fact that he 'fled the country', while dealing with his ownership of land before the Conquest. The most important of these entries deals with Hereward's abortive lease of land in Rippingale, north of Bourne, which he had lost for breaking the terms of his lease. He had made a bargain with the new Abbot of Crowland, Ulfcytel, appointed in 1062, to take the land on an annually renewable lease and almost immediately lost it. This points to 1063 as the most likely year. According to the *Gesta Herewardi* he had various adventures in Northumbria (where he is said to have encountered Gilbert de Gand (or 'of Ghent'), Cornwall and Ireland. These are the stuff of romance and can be compared to such tales as that of

Tristan and Isolde, because he helps the King of Ireland's son win as his bride the King of Cornwall's daughter. Needless to say, in the eleventh century there was no king in Cornwall. He then goes, like so many others exiled from England at this time, to Flanders and that is an entirely different matter. Here the people he encounters are real, and held the positions ascribed to them. His activities fit the pattern of an exile who becomes a mercenary soldier and serves in the campaigns of the period. In Flanders, then, he learnt his trade as a soldier, possibly even the art of fighting on horseback, the distinguishing mark of a knight, which would account for the emphasis in twelfth-century writers on his knightly status.

The story is that after having returned from Ireland and having paid a visit to the Orkneys, Hereward sets off for Flanders and is shipwrecked, possibly by the autumn storms in the Channel, near 'St Bertin', that is the abbey at St Omer, probably late in 1063. There he meets Count Manasses the Old and other great men, is recruited into the army of the Count of Flanders in his war with the Count of Guînes and fights his nephew, called here Hoibricht. At St Omer he meets Turfrida, a wealthy lady who is being courted by the nephew of the lord of St Valéry. He participates in 'military contests' (which seem to be early examples of tournaments) at Bruges and Poitiers, renowned centres of such activity, and performs well. He becomes a *magister militum* and instructs new recruits in the art of war, defeats Hoibricht, marries Turfrida and is joined by his paternal cousins, Siward the White (Blonde) and Siward the Red (Rufus). He then goes on an expedition to 'Scaldemariland' with Robert, son of the Count of Flanders. Robert is attempting to force the people there to pay tribute. On his return to Flanders, Hereward finds that his patron, the count, is dead and his successor has not yet taken up office, so Hereward and his companion, Martin Lightfoot, return to England, leaving the cousins to protect Turfrida.

In England he learns that his father's house and his homeland are 'subject to the rule of foreigners and almost ruined by the exactions of many men'. He drives out the French occupants of his home and avenges the death of his younger brother. He goes to the Abbot of Peterborough, Brand, to seek knighthood at his hands. The abbot confers knighthood on him 'in the English manner' and a monk of Ely called Wulfwine confers it on Hereward's companions. He encounters and kills Frederick, brother-in-law of William de Warenne, somewhere in Norfolk and, wisely perhaps, returns to Flanders. There he rejoins Turfrida and fights on behalf of a most famous knight called Baldwin against the lord of Picquigny. The lord of Brabant is also involved. He then returns again to England, accompanied by his wife and cousins, and takes part in the siege of Ely (and presumably, although the *Gesta Herewardi* does not say so, the attack on Peterborough).

What can be made of all this? Research by Elisabeth van Houts has revealed the facts behind the story. The war in Scaldemariland is a straightforward matter. The *Vita of St Willibrord* by Abbot Theofrid of Echternach states that the saint and his church had land on the Island of Walcheren in the Scheldt Estuary and a miracle story in the *Vita* recounts how the son of Count Baldwin of Flanders attempted to exact taxes from the Islanders, dwelling in the 'Scaldemermur', that is the Scheldt Estuary. The invaders were repulsed in the ensuing fight, thanks to St Willibrord, and their banners were sent to Echternach in thanksgiving. This is the *Gesta Herewardi* story from the other side. The son of Count Baldwin was Robert the Frisian who was himself count from 1071 to 1093. His father, Baldwin V, Duke William's father-in-law, ruled from 1063 to 1071, the period when Hereward was active and Robert was in Flanders and Holland at that time endeavouring to enforce his authority over the region. The area of conflict is variously called 'Scaldemer-mur' or 'Scaldemariensis', referring to the islands in the province of Zeeland later called 'Scoudemarediep' or 'Scaldemer-mur' meaning 'Scheldt-sea' (Scalde = Scheldt plus 'mere', seawater or lake). The *Vita* of the saint talks about Walcheren being on the other side of it and refers to the fortress of Middleburg. The *Gesta Herewardi* speaks of sand-dunes and of a '*Castra Scaldemariensium*' that is the forts of Middleburg, Domburg and Souburg. It is a picture of an area fought over by the princes of the surrounding regions of the Scheldt and Rhine estuaries and the account in the *Gesta Herewardi* supports this picture.

The *Annals of St Bertin* relate that Robert the Frisian entered Frisia in 1063 and other sources relate that he was twice beaten back from Frisia before he became count. The *Gesta Herewardi* suggests a date for all this by saying that it occurred just before the death of the old Count Baldwin V and before Baldwin VI took office. That is before 1 September 1067 when Baldwin VI was still in either Ponthieu or Hainault. Before the expedition Hereward is said to have been at Cambrai. Light is shed on this by a charter of the Bishop of Cambrai, Lietbert 1051–1076, datable to about 1065. The witnesses include one 'Miles Herrivardi'. This could well be Hereward. The name is of Germanic origin known in France but neither French nor Flemish records mention any others at this particular time and the date and place fit. The use of 'v' for 'u' is well documented. The *Gesta Herewardi* also says that Hereward met Manasses the Old of Guînes, who first witnesses a charter in 1056, and his son, another Baldwin, ruled from 1065 to 1091. Guînes is on the estuary of the River Aa which leads to St Omer and the count was responsible for all wrecked ships within his jurisdiction. Hereward on landing was taken to Count Manasses and that dates his arrival to before 1065. He takes part in military contests at Bruges and Poitiers, and the earliest other known reference to such contests is for Poitiers in 1067. The *Gesta Herewardi* calls them 'festive competitions'.

If Hereward was at Cambrai, that would explain his aid given to 'the very famous Baldwin' against the 'Vidame' or Vicomte of Picquigny. The latter would be Arnulf of Picquigny and the Baldwin either Baldwin V or his son Baldwin VI of Hainault. There is no cast-iron proof that Hereward was involved with these people, but it does all fit and makes sense of his exile. St Omer is prominent in the *Gesta Herewardi* and it had strong ties with England. It was a monk of St Bertin, Goscelin, who wrote the *Encomium Emmae* (*In Praise of Queen Emma*, King Edward's mother). Perhaps the material about Flanders in the *Gesta Herewardi* also came from there. Folcard of St Bertin knew Ealdred, Archbishop of York, and became Abbot of Thorney (deposed 1085). Goscelin had spent time at Peterborough, Ely and Ramsey in the 1080s and these facts probably explain the transmission of this information.

St Omer also had connections with Earl Tostig, who was briefly deputy to the castellan of the town, Wulfric Rabel, in 1065. Did his presence there attract Hereward, like other exiles, hoping for the earl's aid in being recalled to England? St Omer was also the refuge, after the Conquest, of Gytha, Harold's mother. It seems more likely to have been in Flanders, not Northumbria, that Hereward first encountered Gilbert of Ghent and perhaps also Frederic Oosterzele-Scheldewindeke, later brother-in-law of Earl William de Warenne. Gilbert is said to have offered Hereward his protection and knighthood, which he refused, and that is more suited to Flanders than Northumbria. The *Gesta Herewardi* could have misplaced this encounter by confusing it with a more hostile meeting between the two in Northumbria in 1069. Frederic's family were hereditary advocates or protectors of St Bertin. Gilbert of Ghent was the younger son of Ralph of Alost or Aalst, advocate of St Peter's, Ghent. Gilbert had lands in Lincolnshire and Northamptonshire and founded Bardney Abbey.

There is one mystery; the identity of Turfrida. It is a continental, not an English name, and she is said to have been a clever and educated woman from a rich family. Perhaps she was the daughter or sister of Wulfric Rabel the castellan. Marriage to such a woman fits the common pattern for mercenaries who tried to marry into the family of a military superior. After the defeat of the rebels at Ely and Hereward's withdrawal, Turfrida is said to have become a nun at Crowland and to have died there after four years. There is also Hereward's alleged second wife, whom Geoffrey Gaimar calls Alftruda. (This looks like the English name Aelfthryth, which had travelled to Flanders after a daughter of Alfred the Great was married to the count.) Alftruda was said to have been wife or widow of Dolfin, eldest son of Cospatrick, Earl of Dunbar. In Gaimar's version of events she outlived Hereward.

After his adventures in Flanders Hereward returned to England and became involved in the attack on Peterborough, then the siege of Ely where the defenders regarded him, according to the *Gesta Herewardi*, as '*princeps et dux eorum*', their chief and commander. This is the subject of earlier chapters. Flanders is important to the development of the Hereward legend. It was the centre or heart of chivalry and knighthood. Fighting there, he learnt to use horse and lance and to fight like a knight. Pre-Conquest thegns were knights in the strict sense of Richard fitzNigel's phrase in the *Dialogus de Scaccario*. A thegn could be an 'active knight', that is '*miles in armis strenuis*', one who 'delights in the glory of arms and takes pleasure in using them'. He has 'the right to be reckoned a man of war' and is equipped with arms and horses. It is also claimed that Hereward was '*magister militum*', that is the officer who, after knights had trained together in groups of five or ten, combined them together into larger units and who also was responsible for the training in arms of the younger knights. But his main function was to command the stipendiary knights or the household troops of his lord.

According to the *Gesta Herewardi*, Hereward escaped after the siege of Ely with a few trusted companions and withdrew to 'the sea called Wide near Welle' where there were ample waterways through which they could escape. This suggests the area near Outwell and Upwell with the Wellstream leading to Wisbech and The Wash. (The Wellstream disappeared after the draining of the Fens.) The Peterborough Register says that Wisbech castle was founded 'on that most famous river which is called Wellstream.' (There is a tradition that it was at Welle that King John lost his treasure.) This idea that Hereward slipped away from the isle before King William's men could catch him is confirmed by the *Peterborough Chronicle*. It seems that he had gone down the Ouse and from there into the Wellstream not far from Peterborough, heading for The Wash. He left some of his men, with orders to lay waste the land with fire, to cover the retreat no doubt, at a place called 'Cissahum' (which could be Chettisham between Ely and Littleport), and they hid on a small island called 'Stimtencia' (which no longer exists following the draining of the Fens), before rejoining Hereward. He remained at large 'on the Wide sea' pursued by local levies raised by King William from Lincolnshire and no doubt was hunted by the king's 'butsecarles' or fighting boatmen. As a result he turned inland towards the forest of 'Brunneswald' located 'in the great woods of Northamptonshire'. This area extends from around Leighton Bromeswold (held before the Conquest by Thorkell of Harringworth, one of Hereward's supporters) along the eastern boundary of Northamptonshire from Ellington to Old Weston, in Huntingdonshire, on to Newton Bromeswold and Lutton. It should, however, be remembered that there is an area of the Isle of Ely, on the high clay ground near Witchford and Witcham, which was also called 'Bruneswold' and place name study shows that the forests extended into that area. Another way to describe the Brunneswald is to locate it along the valley of the Nene River, south of Thorney and west of Ely, north of Bedford and east of Kettering.

The *Gesta Herewardi* insists that King William wanted to hunt Hereward down and that he gathered the levies of nine shires (although only seven are named) to search the northern end of the Brunneswald around Bourne where he was believed to be hiding. Here the chronology of the *Gesta Herewardi* is in error. It brings Hereward up against Turold, Abbot of Peterborough and Ivo Taillebois, Sheriff of Lincolnshire who are leading a combined force of horse and foot soldiers. They fight, and slingers and archers are involved amongst the trees. Hereward is assisted by 'Rahenaldus' or Rainald, said to be his standard bearer and to be steward of Ramsey Abbey. He has not been further identified. Hereward lays waste the town of Peterborough by fire and plunders the treasure of the church. He then 'overtook the abbot although he and his men wished to escape by hiding themselves'.

This appears to confuse the fighting in the Brunneswald with the attack on Peterborough which is thus placed after rather than before the siege of Ely. The account in the *Peterborough Chronicle* and in Hugh Candidus is to be preferred. The *Gesta Herewardi* account says that Turold, along with his nephew and other men, was captured and Hereward is said to have ransomed the abbot for the impossible sum of 30,000 silver marks (£20,000) and allowed his man Siward the White to release him. Taking prisoners for ransom is a very twelfth-century concept, common in France from the mid-eleventh century onwards, but was not practised in England. The English did not take prisoners nor spare warriors in a pitched battle. Of course, Hereward had fought in Flanders and might have learned these conventions while there, but it is unlikely that Turold could have been captured and ransomed without this being mentioned by at least Hugh Candidus. A version of this tale is in the *Annales Burgo-Spaldenses*, which says that Turold took sixty-two hides of the abbey's lands and gave them to his stipendiary soldiers, that is mercenaries who had protected him against 'Hereward le Wake' yet that nonetheless he and many other magnates had been captured by Hereward and ransomed. Under the date AD 1098 it notes Turold's death and again says that he 'enfeoffed' soldiers with land belonging to the abbey and built a castle next door to the abbey and was responsible for many other evil deeds. This castle is said to have been called 'Mount Turold' rather as the motte at Warwick is known as 'Aethelfleda's Mound'. Turold, of course, continues to seek out Hereward. A germ of truth may lie in these accounts. Perhaps there was a confrontation, near Stamford in Lincolnshire, between Hereward and his men and Turold and his, in which Turold came close to capture and escaped. Later story tellers would then have invented the ransom story to suit the taste of twelfth-century audiences. The sixty-two hides come from the additions to Hugh Candidus by Walter of Whittlesey, as does the matter about Mount Turold. Hugh himself simply says that the abbot granted 'many of the possessions of the Church to soldiers on condition that they... supplied forthwith military assistance to subdue Hereward'.

The tale of how Hereward escaped from Ely and hid out in the Brunneswald is also in Geoffrey Gaimar's *L'Estorie des Engles*. He too puts the attack on Peterborough after rather than before the siege of Ely. All these sources are using a version of Hereward's activities, possibly the street ballads, which suffers from these temporal dislocations. Gaimar claims that the attack was in revenge on the monks for their support for King William. There then follows the *Gesta Herewardi* story of how Hereward was warned in a vision by an old man of terrible aspect carrying a large key, an obvious reference to St Peter, who ordered him to restore its treasures to Peterborough. He promises to do so and his reward is to be guided through the marshes by a white dog, which turns out to be a wolf, so avoiding his enemies. His soldiers' lances are lit by what the common folk call 'Fairy Lights', that is the marsh gas effect called Will o' the Wisp. The whole story is meant to show how St Peter, patron saint of Peterborough, protects his church. In reality much of the treasure was lost, some in the Danish ships lost at sea, and other parts remained in Denmark. Some was recovered by the efforts of Prior Aethelwold who had been taken to Denmark by the Danes along with some of his monks. He was particularly concerned to rescue the arm of St Oswald. Some treasure was returned to Ramsey Abbey and Turold recovered it from there. Hereward had nothing to do with it after entrusting it to the 'care' of the Danes. Further accounts of his adventures in the Brunneswald are drawn from the cycle of tales about him which circulated in the early twelfth century. As the *Pseudo-Ingulf* version says, his exploits were 'sung about in the streets'.

The end of his story differs in the two main accounts of his activities, the *Gesta Herewardi* and Geoffrey Gaimar. In Gaimar he is reconciled to the king, at the intercession of the lady Alftruda or Aelfthryth and accompanies him in his war in Maine. It is known that William took English levies with him on that campaign. Then, on Hereward's return he is set upon by a gang of Norman knights, led by a certain Ralph de Dol (which looks like a reference to Ralph de Gael who took refuge in Dol after his exile for participation in the Revolt of the Earls and made war on King William). Hereward kills a surprising number of them, despite being caught unarmed while dining, but is eventually overwhelmed and killed by Ralph, who also dies. The comment is made that if the English had had three men like him the Normans would have been driven out of the country. Gaimar is granting his hero a suitably heroic death and this account cannot be accepted – it is the stuff of romance. Also this death is very like the fate of

Earl Edwin of Mercia who was set upon by twenty-four
Normans and slain and the story may in part be drawing
on that affair.

The *Gesta Herewardi* has a complicated story. Hereward
is again reconciled to the king but slandered by various
jealous Normans and imprisoned at Bedford in the care of
Robert de Horepol (Harpole, a suburb of Northampton
today). He is imprisoned at the insistence of Earl William
de Warenne (whose brother-in-law Frederick was said to
have been slain by Hereward – or his men in an alternative version), Robert Malet and Ivo Taillebois, all enemies
of Hereward from the siege of Ely. Robert de Horepol
reveals that Ivo is planning to have Hereward moved to
Rockingham and allows Hereward to contact his men
through Leofric the Deacon. They rescue Hereward,
taking care not to harm de Horepol or any of his men.
The gaoler agrees to intercede for Hereward with King
William. He does so and convinces him that Hereward
has been unjustly treated and would be a good servant to
the king. William is won over and issues letters confirming Hereward's right to his father's lands. He is received
into the king's peace and serves him for many years.
During all this his wife Turfrida becomes jealous of a rich
woman, Alftruda, who originally persuaded King William
to accept Hereward's submission. Turfrida leaves him and
becomes a nun at Crowland, where she dies. Hereward
then marries Alftruda. Crowland Abbey claimed that
when Hereward finally died he was, like Earl Waltheof,
buried at Crowland. The idea that Hereward survived in
this manner may reflect knowledge of the other Hereward
named in Domesday Book, with lands in Warwickshire
and Worcestershire held of the Bishop of Worcester and
the Count of Mortain and indicate a confusion between
the two. The Warwickshire man was the pre-Conquest
holder of these lands and there is no evidence that he
ever rebelled.

There is really no way to decide between these two contrasting accounts, either from internal evidence or the reliability of the sources. The stories in Gaimar and the *Gesta Herewardi* appear to be products of the early twelfth century. Gaimar wrote in about 1139/40 for Constance, wife of a minor Lincolnshire baron called Ralph fitzGilbert, who could be an unidentified member of the fitzGilbert clan of Tonbridge and Clare. Gaimar used some reliable sources, including a version of the *Anglo-Saxon Chronicle* that has now disappeared which he got from Walter Espec the Yorkshire baron and friend of Robert of Gloucester, Henry I's illegitimate son; and a copy of 'the good book of Oxford by Walter the archdeacon', that is Geoffrey of Monmouth's *History of the Kings of Britain*, which is a romance and not real history at all. Gaimar's purpose was partly to entertain and partly, like the author of the *Gesta*, to make a case favourable to the reputation of the English, still looked down on at that period by those of Norman blood. The *Gesta Herewardi* is at least in part the work of Richard of Ely (not the abbot of that name), who was responsible for large parts of the *Liber Eliensis* but not for the texts that have survived, but he might have written that part which relates to the siege of Ely. The rest is of unknown authorship. Neither Gaimar nor the author of the *Gesta Herewardi* as we have it in Robert of Swaffham's text was writing strict history – each was seeking to entertain his audience and each had his own axe to grind. The *Gesta Herewardi* seeks to convince its readers that the English were noble warriors and fitting opponents for King William. Even the accounts of how Hereward was able to spy on the Normans in disguise are meant to suggest that the Normans could not recognise an English aristocrat when they saw one.

There is an alternative scenario. Perhaps Hereward neither died in a brawl with some Normans nor lived to a ripe old age as a servant of King William. Most of the rebels who survived the fighting and were neither imprisoned by the Normans, like Morcar, nor mutilated like the lesser leaders captured at Ely, went into exile. This appears to have been the fate of Siward Barn, for example. Is it not probable that Hereward, like so many others, simply went into exile? There is a faint clue which gives some colour to this hypothesis. According to the *Historia Ecclesia Eliensis*, a certain 'Hereward' married Wilburga of Terrington, Norfolk and he granted to the church of Lynn one carucate of land with instructions that prayers be said 'for Hereward his father and Hereward the Exile his grandfather'. Here we have a line of descent from 'Hereward the Exile' in the male line to parallel the claims made by the Wake family of descent in the female line. This marriage comes from the reign of Henry II who became king in 1154 and three generations takes us back to 1064. The descent is quite feasible. If Hereward died in exile then no one would know exactly what happened to him and the twelfth-century writers could safely devise their own accounts.

IO

The Heirs of Hereward

THE WAKE FAMILY AND THE RE-EMERGENCE OF
ENGLISHNESS

A permanent result of Charles Kingsley's romance, *Hereward the Wake*, is that everybody knows that Hereward was called 'the Wake'. Yet it is quite certain that the name was never used in his lifetime nor for over a hundred years afterwards. He is not so labelled in any early source, not even by that inveterate gossip Orderic Vitalis. Instead he is known as 'the Outlaw' or 'the Exile' and to 'Florence' of Worcester he is a '*vir strenuus*', that is a 'hard man' who commands the defence of Ely. But never, ever, is he 'the Wake'. The name derives quite simply from the surname of a mid-twelfth-century baronial family, descendants of Hugh son of Geoffrey Wac or Wake, who had become lords of the Lincolnshire barony of Bourne. In the course of the next half century they began to claim descent in the female line from a daughter of Hereward, and so, in due course, Hereward became known as 'the Wake'.

Hugh Wake married well, Emma, the daughter of Baldwin fitzGilbert, and their son was Baldwin Wake, named presumably for his grandfather. By the end of the twelfth century it was becoming fashionable to claim an English ancestor, and for some reason or other, the Wakes, who might have made more of their membership, by marriage, of the family of Tonbridge and Clare, descendants of Count Gilbert of Brionne, fixed on Hereward. Perhaps this was because some of the lands which went to make up the barony of Bourne had once been owned by him, as Domesday Book shows. Yet the barony itself had only been formed in the reign of Henry I.

Baldwin fitzGilbert was a fitzGilbert of Clare, a member of the illustrious clan descended from Richard de Bienfaite or fitzGilbert, of whom collateral descendants include the Earls of Hertford and of Pembroke. Baldwin's father was Richard fitzGilbert, and Richard, Abbot of Ely was his uncle. Richard fitzGilbert himself was second son of Count Gilbert of Brionne and his elder brother was Baldwin, Sheriff of Devon. Count Gilbert was son of Godfrey, illegitimate son of Duke Richard I of Normandy and, before his murder in 1041, tutor to the boy duke, William.

The story of the descent of the barony of Bourne is a clue to the process, still cloaked in darkness, by which Norman lordship spread throughout the county of Lincolnshire in the century following the Conquest, and casts further light on the interesting though little known process by which the holdings of English thegns were subordinated to the fief of a Norman baron. J.H. Round showed that Baldwin fitzGilbert was a Clare, that he was that Baldwin de Clare who addressed the troops on behalf of King Stephen before the Battle of Lincoln in 1141, and that he was son of Gilbert fitzGilbert. He is shown in the Arundel manuscript of

Henry of Huntingdon's History with two Clare chevrons
on his shield and is identified by a marginal note as the
grandfather of Baldwin Wake. It was through him that the
Bourne barony descended to the Wakes.

Henry I formed the 'Honor' of Bourne out of lands in
Lincolnshire, Northamptonshire and Hertfordshire, around
the nucleus of the Bourne fief and gave it to William de
Rullos who had a brother called Richard. These two are
well known as witnesses to various charters of this period
and Richard himself issued a charter (printed in Stenton's
First Century of English Feudalism; Egerton manuscript
2827 f.16) written between 1125 and 1155. It grants land
at Skeeby in Easby, Yorkshire, to one of his men. Richard
was one of the chief barons of Richmondshire, holding his
estates of the Earls of Richmond. It was Adelina, daughter
of Richard de Rullos, who married Baldwin fitzGilbert,
who thus inherited the barony, possibly as his wife's dowry.
Baldwin paid Henry I for his marriage and his lands:

> Baldwin fitz Gilbert renders account of £301 16s 4d. For the
> land of William de Rullos with the daughter of his brother
> Richard. Into the Treasury £35. (Pipe Roll 31 Henry I : 110)

A later story, part of the claim to be descended from
Hereward, is that Richard de Rullos had married a daughter, possibly called Godiva or Godgifu, of a Peterborough
knight called Hugh d'Envermeu, who himself had married
a daughter of Hereward, called, like her mother, Turfrida.
As these marriages cannot be proved it is not certain that
the Wakes are descendants of Hereward. J.H. Round certainly concluded that it was false because the link to Hugh
d'Envermeu is so tenuous. It was to add colour to their
claim of descent from Hereward that the Wakes called
Hereward 'the Wake'.

The descent of the barony is clear enough. It can be
traced very neatly from William and Richard de Rullos

to Baldwin Wake. It is the connection with Hereward that now needs to be considered. Certainly Hereward came from somewhere around Bourne in Lincolnshire, as the pages of Domesday Book show. But what they do not show is any direct connection with Bourne itself. He is not Hereward of Bourne. Domesday Book assigns Bourne to Morcar, Earl of Northumbria and says that after the Conquest it was held by Ogier the Breton. It has been argued that Morcar was only holding Bourne because Hereward had forfeited his land. There is evidence for this sort of thing being done in other cases of outlawry but there is no record of any such forfeiture by Hereward. The suggestion is mere speculation for which there is no evidence. Domesday cheerfully records other lands as actually held by Hereward, and two cases of land said to be his but which he did not hold 'on the day he fled'. If he had had a claim to Bourne it would surely have said so, even if only to dismiss it.

Some of the lands given as owned by Hereward did later form part of the barony of Bourne. He is said to have held Witham-on-the-Hill, Manthorpe, Toft and Lound. He also had an estate at Laughton and it was suggested, but dismissed, that he had land in Barholme. Also land at Rippingale had been his 'at farm' from the abbey of Crowland, but the abbot had taken the land back because Hereward had not kept to his agreement before he 'fled from the country'.

These lands are found listed in several successive lists of the abbey's lands; the *Descriptio Terrarum of Peterborough Abbey*, dated to between 1071 and 1101; the *Descriptio Militum de Abbatia de Burgo*, a list of Peterborough knights, dated between 1110 and 1125 (this states that Hugo de Euremon [d'Envermeu] held lands in Lincolnshire, which included Witham-on-the-Hill and Barholme, given to Asford by Abbot Turold); and the *Descriptio Terrarum*, dated to 1125-27, which lists the four estates of Hereward as

land of the abbey's demesne. The text of Hugh Candidus
asserts that these were held in his own day by Baldwin
Wake. Indeed a charter of Henry I from Rouen *c*.1129
confirms his earlier charter for the Priory of Envermeu
(Seine Inférieur) concerning its lands in England and 'what
Baldwin fitzGilbert granted it out of the land which had
belonged to Hugh of Envermeu'. It shows that Baldwin
now held Hugh's English lands, not how he acquired
them. *The Lindsey Survey* (1115-1118) lists Peterborough
lands which include those saved for the abbey by Abbot
Brand.

There are other lands included in the *Honor of Bourne*
which can also be found in Domesday Book: obviously
Bourne itself, and Rippingale, both held by Ogier the
Breton. Richard de Rullos, according to the *Leicester
Survey*, 1124-29, held land at Thorpe and Twyford once
held by Ogier. The lands at Barholme and Stow were
given as Asfort's land in the *Descriptio Terrarum* and were
part of the abbey demesne in the later surveys. These also
were held by Baldwin Wake. The full tradition is found in
Walter of Whittlesey's thirteenth-century additions to the
text of Hugh Candidus (B.Mus. Add. MS 39758) where
he says that Baldwin Wake held land in Deeping, Plumtree
and Stowe for a fee of two knights and had one knight's
fee in Witham-on-the-Hill and Barholme 'of the land of
Asford' for which he owed the Abbot of Peterborough full
service. This shows the way in which Henry I gathered up
a number of estates in and around Bourne, with other scattered lands elsewhere, and bundled them together as part
of the barony of Bourne. It so happened that a number of
them had belonged to Hereward and had been held by a
Norman knight, Asfort, who was his successor. This does
not, of course, explain why the Wakes claimed descent from
Hereward. It is true that other Norman lords are known to
have married the heiresses, whether widows or daughters,
of the thegns who were their 'antecessores', that is who had

held the lands they now possessed. It may be that it was thought that this made their ownership look more legitimate in the eyes of the English. It is, therefore, possible that Hugh d'Envermeu married a daughter of Hereward, but in the absence of better evidence this remains improbable. Nor is there any direct record of how Hugh came to hold his estates. The only evidence for this alleged marriage comes from a very late and often untrustworthy source, the *Pseudo-Ingulf*, which certainly had access to genuine sources, some of which can be identified, but the author used his sources very badly and made numerous quite ridiculous mistakes. Where he cannot be verified, what he says must be treated with caution. It is he who asserts that Hereward's daughter Turfrida married Hugh d'Envermeu, whom he calls Hugo de Evermue, Lord of Deeping and Bourne and that her daughter married Richard de Rullos, described as the king's chamberlain (sub anno 1076). Richard was no such thing. *Pseudo-Ingulf* also gives a very garbled account of Hereward's parentage which seems to derive from the same source as the account in the *Gesta Herewardi*. The case cannot be said to be proven. The Wakes certainly did well out of their alliance with the House of Clare and later in the century created their own family myth to support their claim to the barony and a noble English ancestry.

Both Hugh d'Envermeu and the de Rullos brothers can be identified a little more closely. Hugh was from Envermeu, ten miles from Dieppe. He was, according to French records, a benefactor of the abbey of Bec (as were several members of the Clare family in Henry I's time) and gave it the Priory of St Laurent d'Envermeu. Hugh's connection with Baldwin fitzGilbert through the de Rullos brothers is confirmed by King Henry's confirmation in 1129 for the Priory of St Laurent of Envermeu of 'what Baldwin fitzGilbert granted it of the land which had belonged to Hugh of Envermeu'. Hugh witnesses two writs in 1106, and a charter in 1111, and is the subject of a charter issued between 1102 and 1107 in which he restores the manor of Doddington to St Peter of Westminster in exchange for Duxford.

William and Richard de Rullos are identifiable from charter evidence. They came from Roullours, Calvados. Richard gave the church of Roullours to the Priory of St Stephen at Plessis-Grimoult c.1126-29 and the Pipe Roll of Henry I shows that he was 'recently dead' by 1130. King Henry confirms a gift of land by William de Rullos to the church of Bec in 1115. William witnesses five writs in Henry's reign. The brothers are said to have been chamberlains but this cannot be so. There was a William the Chamberlain under William I. He is given no other name and is not one of the other Williams who held the office at that time. The brothers are not found named as holding the office of chamberlain under either William Rufus or Henry I. As for Hugh Wake, he was chief lieutenant in Lincolnshire of Rannulf Gernons, Earl of Chester, witnessing a charter of his c.1145. According to his return in the *Carta Baronum* of 1166 he held ten and ⅛ knight's fees.

So the Wake claim to descent from Hereward is a doubtful one although they certainly held lands in the second half of the twelfth century which Domesday Book records as having belonged to or been associated with him. What the record shows is the process by which lands passed from holder to holder, the role that marriage played in this process, and that baronies might be formed out of groups of scattered estates belonging in Domesday Book to a variety of lords, holding the lands of specific pre-Conquest earls and thegns.

This question of the claim to descent from Hereward by the Wakes raises an altogether separate and more interesting one, and that concerns the nature of the process by which 'Englishness' reasserted itself. During the reigns of the Conqueror and his son William Rufus the English were regarded and treated as a subject people, yet from the

middle of the reign of Henry I, second and third generation Norman settlers were beginning to refer to England
as their homeland and by the time of the Battle of the
Standard, in Northumbria in 1138 against the Scots, those
Englishmen writing about it can be found boasting that
'our boys' (*nostri*) won. One reason for the depression of
the English, quite apart from the loss of estates by the
former landowning classes, was that many English families
became extinct even before William I's coronation through
the death of heirs in one of the three battles of 1066. Edwin
and Morcar's force at Fulford was almost annihilated in a
murderous and protracted battle. At both Stamford and
Hastings where the burden was on the retainers of Harold
and his brothers and the thegns of Wessex and eastern
England, many thousands died. The Norwegian king
had not been easily defeated then Hastings was a long
drawn out defensive engagement. Add in the effects of the
revolts between 1067 and 1071, and it becomes evident that
many more died, possibly more than in the three battles
themselves. Orderic points out that there was an easy victory at Stafford which may conceal a battle fought on a
considerable scale. Then there were the effects of exile
and emigration in which so many fled to Denmark and
many 'good men' went to Scotland. Those who went to
Denmark have left little trace but in Scotland the charters
of Malcolm and his sons reveal many English personal
names and place names.

As is revealed by a consideration of the role and identity of the collaborators and quislings, some men, mainly
of modest means, did survive the Conquest, like Alfsi
of Faringdon's son in Oxfordshire. He was Alewi who
held Milton under Wychwood of Roger d'Ivri in 1086.
His father had held Littleworth near Faringdon under
Harold, Earl of Wessex. Alewi's grandson was Robert
of Astrop, a tenant of the d'Ivri Honor of St Valéry, and
he gave Milton to Bruern Abbey. The grandson bears a

Norman name. This became common in the late eleventh
and early twelfth centuries. Another example is Eadnoth
the Staller's son Harding, in Bristol, whose son was the
portreeve Robert in Matilda's time. The Lords of Berkeley
in Gloucestershire claimed descent from him. The Pipe
Roll of Henry I has some fifteen or more examples of the
survival of Englishmen and women and such names occur
as Osbert fitzColegrim, Atscelina wife of Robert Fossard,
and Haimo fitzAtsor (or Azor) of Marlborough whose
father is called 'Atsor the Englishman' and is claimed as
the ancestor of the Ridware family. Henry of Oxford, a
sheriff in 1154, was son of Godwine son of Eilwi. As well
as direct descent of this kind, marriage to the daughter
or widow of an English family could produce a Norman
dynasty with English blood in its veins. Geoffrey de la
Guerche's wife was Aelfgifu and it was through her that
he acquired his Midlands estates from her father, the thegn
Leofwine. However, not all such marriages were voluntary and Archbishop Lanfranc himself testifies that some
women were driven to take refuge in convents to avoid a
forced marriage. These marriages began as early as 1068.
One may be allowed to wonder whether the story of
Turfrida becoming a nun at Crowland actually derives
from her need to seek refuge after the death or exile of
Hereward.

Lucy 'the Countess' is a famous character. She lived into
the reign of Henry I and survived three husbands; Ivo
Taillebois or Cut-bush, Roger fitzGerold and Hugh, Earl
of Chester. Her exact parentage is still not fully accounted
for but the most likely explanation is that she was daughter
of Thorold or Turold 'of Lincoln' and that he was Turold,
Sheriff of Lincolnshire (though this latter identification
is disputed). It was once said that she was daughter of
Aelfgar, Earl of Mercia, and she certainly held his manor
of Spalding, but this claim cannot be true as all his children
are accounted for. That her father was named Turold is

certain. When Ivo and Lucy gave land at Spalding for the
foundation of a Priory of St Nicholas of Angers, Ivo said
that the gift was made 'for himself and his wife and their
ancestors, viz. Thorold and his wife'. Furthermore, near the
end of her life, Lucy gave Spalding manor to St Nicholas,
Spalding for the souls of herself and her family. She also
held lands belonging to Turold, as for instance Alkborough
which had previously been the property of William Malet.
She was said to be the niece of Robert Malet of Eye.
The connection is explained if her father was Turold of
Bucknall, the sheriff, because he was married to Beatrix,
daughter of William Malet, whose brother was Robert
Malet. Through Lucy and her marriages, the Earls of both
Lincoln and Chester can be shown to have had English
ancestors. One other matter of some interest about Lucy
is that the tower of Lincoln Castle was known as Lucy's
Tower, no doubt because, as a charter of King Stephen
issued for Rannulph, Earl of Chester testifies, Lucy his
mother 'firmavit', that is strengthened or fortified, the tower
of the castle. Intriguingly, one of Hereward's men, called
Acer Vasus or 'the Hard' claimed that his father owned the
tower of the city (of Lincoln). Perhaps his father also was
called Turold.

Lincoln also provides another example of the survival
of English blood. Coleswein of Lincoln, the collaborator
or quisling, who did so well out of the Conquest, had two
children, Picot and Muriel. His daughter married Robert
de la Hay and their son and daughter were Richard and
Cecily. Both Robert de la Hay and Richard became con-
stables of Lincoln Castle and it may be that Coleswein also
had a similar role. Richard de la Hay was dispossessed of
lands and office by King Stephen but restored to both in
1156 by Henry II.

Many men of lesser rank also survived, such as the leading men on the Canterbury estates in London. These were
Englishmen who believed the assurances of King William,

submitted to him and were guaranteed the enjoyment of their fathers' property and rights. English personal names survive among these men even though Norman names were becoming popular, especially, for example, the name Latimer (or Latiner, i.e. interpreter). In Lincoln also names began to change from English to Norman, as for instance William, son of Ougrim; Walter, son of Wulmer and Robert, son of Suartebrand. It became eccentric to retain English names but some did so nevertheless, like Godwin Wigot or Osbert son of Turgar. The first Mayor of Lincoln was Eilsi (Alsige) but his sons all had Norman names. Yet Turgar was mayor c.1150 and his sons were Warner of Hunsgate and Osbert. The leading families of tradesmen and burgesses, despite their Norman names, can be shown to have descended from Englishmen.

A much neglected area of study which casts light on the survival of English customs and belief lies also in the survival of what ecclesiastical archaeology terms 'Saxon' churches. While it is true that the Norman clergy set out to replace English with Norman church architecture, it is also true that this concerned, in the main, the major churches, cathedrals and monastic churches, which were replaced in their entirety by the Norman version of Romanesque, almost as though all traces of their English past had to be eradicated. But the village churches, as modern investigation shows, were retained for some decades before changes of architectural fashion remodelled them. Native styles continued, smaller local churches in the Saxon style were built or survived and native craftsmen added ornamentation in the impressive but severe Norman buildings. It is now known that many more churches retained Saxon features which can still be seen. The tower of Campsall church, South Yorkshire is Saxon with Norman additions, St Peter, Barton-upon-Humber is one of the most complete surviving Saxon churches and the towers of Sompting, Sussex and Earls Barton, Northamptonshire are characteristically

Saxon. In Norfolk, and to a lesser extent in Suffolk, are the region's characteristic Saxon round towers, several of which, notably East Lexham, near Swaffham (possibly the oldest in England), St Mary, Burnham Deepdale, and St Peter at Forncett, are fine examples to which can be added the square tower of St Andrew's, Great Dunham. In this last church the interior is certainly pre-Conquest. Domesday Book casts light on these churches. Sompting had been the property of Earl Leofwine, Earl's Barton that of Bondi the Staller and passed to Countess Judith from Earl Waltheof, and the great thegn Ulf Fenisc held Barton-upon-Humber and the church is mentioned in his entry in Domesday Book. East Lexham's church is also recorded and was held by a thegn called Fathir. Forncett church was held by Colman from Archbishop Stigand and Great Dunham, held by Pain in 1066, was held from his son Edmund by Reginald the priest and an unnamed daughter of Pain himself. Burnham Deepdale, held by an unnamed thegn in 1066, passed to the great baron Roger Bigod, Sheriff of Norfolk.

As clerical writers demonstrate, English names might be retained alongside a Norman one. Orderic repeatedly insists that he is 'Vitalis the Englishman' and it is he, after not only the Conqueror but also his son William Rufus were safely dead, who calls William 'the Bastard'. The *Textus Roffensis* supplies examples of men with two names, such as '*Ulfuuardus cognomine Henricus de Hou*' or Wulfweard of Hoo called Henry. The poet 'Adgar' writes, 'I am pleased to name myself; my name is Edgar, but I know something else too; most people call me William' (*Le Gracial* lines 25-34). Other examples of the use of both an English and a Norman name include William Leofric, Eadsige Gerold, and Stephen Harding. There was also Robert the Englishman of Fordham. Even John of Worcester was of mixed blood and William of Malmesbury insists that 'the blood of both peoples flows in

my veins'. His history is a partly unconscious protest by the
conquered against the parvenu Normans who had no
respectable history of which they could boast. It is also
the case that the name Hereward can be found surfac-
ing in the latter part of the twelfth century and into the
thirteenth. There was Hereward husband of Wilburga of
Terrington, who claimed the name as that of his father and
grandfather, and the three brothers at Bury St Edmunds,
Walter, Alexander and Hereward, from the period 1156–80;
then there was Herewardus de Barneby in 1219 and from the
Pipe Roll 33 Henry III 'And for one mark from Hereward
of Hunesworth for false witness' in the account of Sheriff
Thomas Noel. There were also Herewards at Pebwith,
Norfolk, under Henry III. Perhaps the adoption of the name
Hereward, as also of other English names, indicates at least a
tendency to look back to the golden age of King Edward.

This respect for their English forebears and lost English
history is shown in the literary affectations of those writers
who sought to revive or satisfy an interest in the English
past. Geoffrey Gaimar, writing in French, calls his work
L'Estorie des Engles, the History of the English, and Henry
of Huntingdon calls his the *Historia Anglorum*. Other writers betray a knowledge of Old English, not only Orderic
but Henry of Huntingdon, Gervase of Canterbury, Ralph
of Howden (probably an hereditary parson of Howden
in Yorkshire), Simeon of Durham and Walter Map. They
allow respect for England to show through in their writing
as when the Battle of the Standard is fought and won by
'English magnates' like Walter Espec as members of the
'*Exercitus Anglorum*' or Army of the English. Henry I when
moving to expel Robert of Bellême from the kingdom in
1102 raised both the feudal levy of knights and the English
fyrd as the army of the whole of England.

Ailred of Rievaulx stresses Henry II's royal pedigree
through his grandfather Henry I and his wife Edith-Matilda
in his *Genealogica Regum Anglorum*. In 1163 in writing a

commentary on Edward the Confessor's famous vision of
the Green Tree (from the *Vita Edwardi Regis*), he stresses
that there were now English abbots, bishops and nobles
and a king of English stock so that the tree which had been
divided was now reunited. This had been foreshadowed
by Orderic who emphasised that Edgar the Aetheling and
several others of the royal line were, as he put it, 'according
to the laws of the Hebrews and other peoples' nearer heirs
to the English crown than any Norman. Even at the end
of William I's reign there had been still some recognition
of Edgar's rights regarding the throne. The Chroniclers
hint at it. Henry of Huntingdon says of the year 1087 that
'there was now no prince of the ancient royal race living
in England' and the *Anglo-Saxon Chronicle* for 1100 calls
Henry I's wife Edith-Matilda a member of 'the rightful
kingly line'. She was Edgar's niece.

It is against this background, of a revival of the con-
sciousness not only of English history but also of English
ancestry, that claims to English descent by prominent families in Henry II's reign and after must be set. J.H. Round
originally demonstrated the English ancestry of several
families, mainly in Northumbria and Mercia. These were
areas laid waste during the rebellions of 1068-1071 and
thus unattractive to Norman settlers. This allowed English
families to retain at least some of their lands and their
identity. Round lists Audley, FitzWilliam of Sprotborough
and FitzWilliam of Hinderskelf, Greystoke, Stanley and
Neville of Raby. This last named adopted the name Neville
in the thirteenth century, when Robert son of Meldred
(Maldred) son of Dolfin son of Uhtred took his wife's name.
This looks like a descent from a twelfth-century member
of the House of Bamburgh. The Yorkshire Domesday itself
lists some thirty-two Englishmen still holding 'in chief'
of the crown who held their land in 1066. So, although
Ailnoth of Canterbury, in his *History of St Cnut, the
King*, says that English magnates had been slain, others

imprisoned, others deprived of their inherited wealth and position, and yet others driven far from their native land while the remainder were oppressed by public servitude, all was not lost. In time the sons and grandsons of Englishmen learned the Norman art of war and became knights and by the middle of Henry I's reign the way opened for English families which had survived the shock of Conquest, to rise again. So in later decades we find substantial numbers of landowners bearing English names or claiming English ancestry, whose property had been inherited and many families which can trace their descent from English thegns rose to great prosperity. It is indeed easier to demonstrate English descent for some families than it is to prove that a particular family actually 'came with the Conqueror', with descent from one of those who fought at the Battle of Hastings.

Although it is therefore true that the rebels were routed and all resistance crushed, yet in the long run it was the English who overcame the Normans in a silent revolution.

II

The Protagonists

The leading protagonists in the Norman Conquest were William the Bastard (both literally and figuratively), Duke of Normandy, the Pretender, and Harold Godwinson, Earl of Wessex and King of England by grant of his predecessor King Edward the Confessor. As Harold died at Hastings there was no English king to lead the continuing struggle against the Normans, and leadership by default fell upon Edgar the Aetheling and the Earls Edwin of Mercia and Morcar of Northumbria. The English therefore divided into a set of collaborators and quislings who took the Norman side, and a motley collection of displaced and disinherited earls and thegns on the side of the Resistance. The obvious candidate for the throne, Edgar the Aetheling, that is, Prince and Heir Apparent, was never actually crowned, partly because the archbishops took the Norman side.

But there was far more resistance than is found in most histories of the Conquest and King William's hold on

England remained insecure until opposition had been over-come. In order to follow the events described in this book, it is useful to have some idea who the many participants were and why they were important. Many of the most vital events were dependent upon the motives and actions of men in various parts of the country who are barely mentioned in standard descriptions of the Conquest. They fall into two main groups, the leaders of the Resistance forming one; leading collaborators the other. A brief note on each of the major Resistance leaders enables estimation of the real strength of the opposition to the Normans.

LEADERS OF THE RESISTANCE

Edgar 'the Aetheling'

He was so called as a potential candidate for the throne; Aetheling means 'of the noble kin', a member of the extended royal family. He was son of Edward the Exile who was himself the son of Edmund Ironside, brother of King Athelred II Unraede (or No Counsel, a pun on Aethelred meaning 'noble-counsel', whom the Victorians called 'the Unready'). Edgar had been brought back from Hungary with his father (who promptly died before his cousin King Edward could welcome him). In 1066 Edgar was still only a youth. Orderic Vitalis said that he became a close friend of Robert Curthose, the Conqueror's son, and that they were almost like brothers, and therefore of much the same age. He could only have been about fourteen years of age in 1065, which explains why he was passed over in favour of Harold Godwinson when King Edward died. He was obviously considered too young to lead a country facing the crisis of 1066. Furthermore he had no close kin to support his claim, was seen as foreign, having been brought up in Hungary, and had not been in England long enough to have built up a network of thegns and sokemen beholden to him. Indeed, he seems to have held little if any land and to have been King Edward's pensioner. Not surprisingly, Harold and the Earls Edwin and Morcar, together with the leading churchmen, ignored his claim.

After his own coronation, William of Normandy heaped honours on Edgar, according to William of Poitiers, and was said to have regarded him as his 'dear companion', because he was a kinsman of King Edward, and to console him for the loss of the crown. He was taken to Normandy with a number of others to share in William's triumph.

As a result of his involvement in revolt Edgar lost almost all the lands he had allegedly received and Domesday Book credits him with little land before 1066 and even less by 1086. That he went into revolt suggests that he had been discontented with his lot and in 1086 he again withdrew from William's court 'because he did not have enough honour from him'. This could well have been the case also in 1068 when he first fled to Scotland.

He played no obvious part in the first rising of 1068, which was the work of the Earls Edwin and Morcar and possibly of Earl Cospatrick son of Maldred. There was insufficient time for Edgar to have become involved. After Whitsun that year Edgar went to Scotland and Orderic, well-informed as ever, maintains that King Malcolm had been preparing an invasion from there on his behalf which was forestalled by his arrival. He may have intended to go to York, but William got there first.

In 1069 his role, like the revolt itself, was very different. This time Edgar was titular head of the invading host which came down from Scotland because he outranked the other leaders, two earls and a sheriff. He would then have been about seventeen, quite old enough to play his part. There seems to have been a half-formed intention to create an Anglo-Danish kingdom in the North, with Edgar as client king to Swein, King of Denmark, on the assumption that William might find central and southern England as much as he could handle and therefore would leave the North to itself. After all, in 1065, the Northumbrians and Yorkshiremen, supported by Edwin, Earl of Mercia, had successfully intimidated King Edward and Harold Godwinson into granting their demands, especially recognition of their own choice of earl. In 1069 the northerners probably thought they could repeat their success, which would explain their use of the usual Northumbrian tactic of raiding deep into enemy territory while avoiding a pitched battle, so that they lived to fight another day. A possible coronation of Edgar by Archbishop Ealdred of York was frustrated by that archbishop's death.

William's prompt and savage reaction shattered the Anglo-Danish coalition and the harrying which followed succeeded in making a renewal of the fighting impossible. The severity of his response suggests that William regarded the rebellion as a serious threat and that he for one did not see Edgar as a mere cypher. In 1071, after settling the matter of Ely, King William invaded Scotland, to end Malcolm's support for the exiles, resulting in Edgar taking refuge in Flanders, only returning to Scotland in 1074.

In that year he accepted an offer from King Philip of France of the use of Montreuil-sur-Mer as a base from which to attack Normandy, but Edgar's fleet was wrecked in a storm so he lost the major portion of his followers and had to accept King Malcolm's advice (and that of his wife Margaret, Edgar's sister) to sue for peace. King William accepted his renewed submission as, with the loss of so many men, Edgar was no longer a threat. That seems to have ended his ambitions and he never recovered his lost prestige. The invitation to return to Scotland was undoubtedly tied in with Malcolm's similar offer of a refuge to Earl Cospatrick, who joined Malcolm's court as Earl of Dunbar.

Edgar spent the next ten years largely in the company of Robert Curthose, thereby forfeiting William's friendship because he and his son were at loggerheads. In 1086 Edgar went to Apulia with some 200 knights to seek fame and fortune, with little success, and on his return in 1089 became one of Robert's chief counsellors. His last adventure was to accompany Robert in the First Crusade, leading the English contingent. He was back in England in Henry I's reign and he died in 1125.

Earls Edwin and Morcar

The next most important members of the leadership should be taken as a pair because they are, as brothers, so often bracketed together in the sources. They were the sons of Aelfgar, Earl of Mercia (and previously of East Anglia) who was the son of Earl Leofric of Mercia and his wife Godiva (Godgifu). Their elder brother Burgheard died in 1062. Their sister, Ealdgyth, married firstly Gruffydd ap Llewelyn of Gwynedd (slain by his compatriots) and secondly in 1066 King Harold to cement his alliance with the earls. As all descendants of Earls Leofric and Aelfgar are accounted for, there is no possibility of any connection with Hereward the Outlaw.

Edwin succeeded his father as Earl of Mercia, possibly in 1063 (the exact year of Aelfgar's death is unknown but Edwin was acting as earl by 1064 and Aelfgar is last heard of on the occasion of his son Burgheard's death). Morcar, at the demand of the rebels against Earl Tostig Godwinson, was accepted as Earl of Northumbria in 1065. The military reputation of the earls never recovered from the overwhelming defeat of their levies at Gate Fulford by Harald Hardrada.

After the Battle of Hastings, in which they took no part, they were at first prepared to support the Aetheling's claims but then agreed with the rest of the Witan to the submission at Berkhamstead. They were among those taken to Normandy in 1067.

Thereafter their resentment against King William grew and festered and they joined the rebels in 1068 but seem to have kept out of the Rising of 1069. Becoming aware that William intended to imprison them, they fled from court in late 1070 or early 1071 and ended up at Ely by autumn of that year.

Earl Cospatrick, son of Maldred

This man was the leading scion of the House of Bamburgh, former Earls of Northumberland. Through his mother, Ealdgyth (granddaughter of King Aethelred), he was descended from the patriarch of the clan, Uhtred, Earl of Northumberland, which made him a relative of Edward the Confessor and, distantly, a member of the English Royal House. Cospatrick was also, through Uhtred, related to Siward, Earl of Northumbria and his son Earl Waltheof, and was cousin to Osulf, son of Eadwulf, the real power in the North before he was killed in 1067, and slayer of Copsige.

Cospatrick's decision to join the rebellion of 1069 seems to have been a matter of impulse. He had already surrendered the earldom he had purchased from King William after the murder of Copsige. Perhaps he realised that he could never make his Northumbrians pay the extortionate *geld* (land tax) demanded by the Conqueror. He, therefore, joined the Aetheling and others in the attack on York. After the defeat of the rising, the earl sued for peace and was reconciled, at a safe distance, to King William. When King Malcolm agreed to the Treaty of Abernethy in 1072, Cospatrick was exiled for a time, returning in 1074 to become Earl of Dunbar, having lost his Northumbrian earldom for being 'on the side of the enemy when the Normans were slain at York'.

Earl Waltheof

Waltheof, son of Earl Siward of Northumbria, was a northerner, despite his possession of an earldom in the East Midlands comprising Northamptonshire, Huntingdonshire and Bedfordshire (and perhaps Cambridgeshire also). He had been too young to become his father's successor in 1055 and had been passed over in favour of Tostig Godwinson.

Through his father's marriage to a granddaughter of Earl Uhtred of the House of Bamburgh, he was cousin to Earl Cospatrick.

After Hastings he had submitted, with many others, accepting William's assurances of good government and confirmation of his status as earl. He too went to Normandy in 1067. He is found witnessing the king's early charters and writs until in 1069 he joined the northern rebellion. He was at York with the Aetheling and distinguished himself in the fighting but after the failure of the rebellion he again submitted to the Norman king, married William's niece, Judith, and accepted the earldom of Northumbria. After the capture of Ely, Waltheof was given many of the estates forfeited by the rebels. He was to remain in office until his involvement in the Rising of the Earls in 1075, for which he was beheaded.

The House of Bamburgh

In the next rank of leadership, below the level of the earls, come various members of the House of Bamburgh, with its supporters and rivals. This great Northumbrian house took its rise from Waltheof I (965-1006), after whom Earl Waltheof was named. Waltheof of Bamburgh's son Uhtred was married three times and through his marriages formed a dynasty which remained powerful in the North until the coming of the Normans. Eadwulf of Bamburgh's brother Cospatrick son of Sige was murdered at King Edward's court, for the alleged benefit of Earl Tostig, a killing which helped to trigger the rising against Tostig. Various members of this house were to involve themselves in opposition to the Normans and took part in the Rising of 1069.

The Clerks of Durham and its Bishops

These Clerks were not monks but secular canons. They were well-connected men with well-to-do relatives, making them a focus of English dynastic power in the region, controlling a considerable block of territory. Their devotion to St Cuthbert and his relics made them a powerful symbol of Northumbrian independence.

The pre-Conquest bishop, Aethelric, had found life in Northumbria hard and violent and saw its people as evil men who often infringed what he saw as the liberty of the Church. So he had taken his chance to retire in favour of his brother, Aethelwine, and went back to live out his time at Peterborough. After the Conquest he was arrested by King William and sent to Westminster to be held in custody there. After this arrest, Aethelric's brother Aethelwine fled to Scotland, so that Aethelric's arrest was the cause not the result of Aethelwine's flight. It may be that Aethelwine was more involved in the northern revolt than appears. When he fled he intended to seek exile in Cologne but a storm wrecked his ship and his plans and he ended up in Scotland. Once there he joined up with Siward Barn and sailed down to meet Earl Morcar at Ely. His exact role is difficult to work out. As bishop he had been sent by King William to negotiate with Malcolm of Scotland in 1069 but the results did not please the king who seems to have distrusted Aethelwine thereafter.

The Sons of Karli and the Thegns of York

Others who rallied to the rebel cause included men with connections with York, particularly the Sons of Karli or Carl, the Hold of York. These were Thorbrand, who had his hall at Settrington in the North Riding, Gamall who shared an estate at Duggleby with his elder brother, Cnut, who also had land in Holderness (which fell into the hands of William Malet 'without the king's writ or seal') and Sumarlithr with land at Crambe. These men joined the attack on York after the murder of Robert de Commines. They were all wealthy men who stood to lose much from the Norman incursion. Thorbrand's lands passed to Berengar de Tosny along with those taken from Gamall.

Carl, and two younger sons, also had wide estates. They survived the rising but lost much of their land. Another who was involved, described by Orderic Vitalis as 'the most powerful of the Northumbrians', was Arnkell son of Ecgfrith who married Sigrid, granddaughter of Bishop Aldun of Durham. Their son, another Cospatrick, was sent, with the keys of the city, as a hostage to William. Arnkell and his son had many manors, and Cospatrick the son still retained many of them even in 1086 though his father was exiled after the rising.

Men from Lincolnshire and East Anglia

The most prominent rebel from Lincolnshire was Maerleswein the sheriff. He was a rich thegn with lands in Lincolnshire (eight manors and a house at Lincoln), Northamptonshire, and Yorkshire. But he also held land in the West Country in Gloucestershire, Somerset and Devon and it is likely that he was involved in some way with the risings there. After 1070 his lands went to Ralph Paynel. He had certainly left Somerset before Matilda's coronation on 11 May 1068, which suggests an involvement at Exeter and connects that revolt with the later risings. It was in 1068 that he joined the Aetheling in Scotland.

He was primarily a northerner and had been left in charge of the North by King Harold after the defeat of Earls Edwin and Morcar, and so escaped the fighting at Stamford Bridge and Hastings. He was one of the leaders who returned from Scotland with the Aetheling in 1068.

Like Earl Cospatrick, Maerleswein had preferred battle to trying to tax the men of the North but after the collapse of the rising he hastily returned to Scotland where he remained at large to foment further revolts. He was thus part of the army which swept down from the North after the murder of de Commines in 1069 but when the Danes retreated before William's advance, Maerleswein found it politic to retreat with Edgar and Siward Barn to

Wearmouth and from there to Scotland. He seems never to have returned to England.

The other most prominent figure with estates in Lincolnshire is Siward Barn or Bearn. He appears for the first time as an associate of Edgar and Maerleswein at Wearmouth and must, therefore, have been involved in the revolt. He had great estates in Lincolnshire, though not all references to 'Siward' in Domesday Book can refer to the same man. Most of his land was in the Midlands, in Nottinghamshire, Derbyshire and Warwickshire. He had an estate in Yorkshire and was rated as one of those with lordly jurisdiction (sake and soke) in Nottinghamshire and Lincolnshire. He must be carefully distinguished from other thegns named Siward, especially Siward son of Aethelgar, a member of the House of Bamburgh and Siward of Maldon who was one of Hereward's men. Siward Barn was rich and of noble birth with lands in seven shires. His confiscated lands went to Henry de Ferrers.

In 1071 he came to Ely with Earl Morcar, seeking to winter there before going into exile. Imprisoned after the siege, he was released by King William on his death bed. *The Sagas* claim that he went to Byzantium under the name 'Sigurd', but this is uncertain and his real fate is unknown.

There are a number of other known rebels with little further information about them, who illustrate the spread and extent of the revolt. A thegn named Skalpi with land in Essex, Norfolk and Suffolk who was a huscarl of King Harold's, 'died in outlawry at York'. Alwine son of Northmann, a thegn from York, was at Wearmouth with the Aetheling and in Scotland. His lands went to Gilbert Tison. There were three East Anglians, Eadric, the steersman of St Benet at Holme; Ringulf of Oby, a man of St Benet's; and Aethelsige of St Augustine's, Canterbury, the administrator of Ramsey Abbey; all three were exiles at the court of King Swein of Denmark.

Archbishop Stigand

The archbishop does not fit exactly into either category. Certainly, he submitted almost immediately to King William, hoping no doubt to secure his position as archbishop, yet he also has definite connections with the rebel side.

He had always been a highly political animal and a dedicated clerical careerist who worked his way up from a position as head of King Edward's secretariat, though without any official title. He became successively Bishop of Elmham (handing it to his brother Aethelmaer) and then Winchester and was elevated to the See of Canterbury after the flight into exile of Robert of Jumièges. But five successive Popes refused to recognise him as archbishop. Only the Anti-Pope Benedict X sent him a pallium. King Harold took good care to be crowned by Archbishop Ealdred of York to avoid any suspicion that his coronation was invalid.

After the Battle of Hastings, Stigand joined others in pressing the Aetheling's claims but then met William at Wallingford and was one of the first to submit. Perhaps he hoped to win William's support by making himself useful to him. But William also chose to have Ealdred perform his coronation, although allowing Stigand to continue in office for the time being.

Stigand was of East Anglian origin, probably from Norwich, and held estates in Cambridgeshire and Huntingdonshire. He was patron of Ely Abbey and deposited his treasure there while on a visit in 1070.

His part in the Resistance is purely circumstantial. The Prior of Canterbury, Aethelsige, went to Denmark (not returning until 1080) and was possibly sent by Stigand to seek the assistance of King Swein in the rebellion. If that were so it would explain King William's decision to have Stigand deposed. If Stigand feared the loss of his wealth, following William's decision to search all the monasteries and confiscate all treasure deposited in them, that would explain his sending Aethelsige to Swein, who arrived in the Humber later that year. That seems to be the sum total of Stigand's involvement.

THE COLLABORATORS

King William's successful takeover of the Old English State and its administrative machine was only possible because of the collaboration and co-operation he secured from the great churchmen, particularly the bishops (the abbots were less co-operative) and from the 'administrative class' of stallers, sheriffs and members of the royal household, headed by the clerk, Regenbald. Because all these men were prepared to put themselves at William's disposal, the whole Old English governmental machine, the most advanced in Europe, swung its weight behind him and many 'patriotic' Englishmen were prepared to work for the new regime. William made them believe that he wanted a genuine Anglo-Norman State although this was never a possibility because the members of his army expected to be rewarded, which meant dispossessing the deluded English. The Old English State was organised by shire and hundred in such a way that every man had a lord and so could be reached by justice and taxed. The system of government became, in William's hands, a means of expropriation of both wealth and land, which was transferred to Norman lords.

Therefore, despite the provocations offered almost daily by the Norman baronage and soldiery, the bulk of the population of southern England, many of whom would have been mourning the loss of fathers, sons and brothers, accepted William's rule and remained quiet.

Bishops were a vital part of the system of government, chosen as much for their administrative abilities or diplomatic skills as for their churchmanship and sanctity. Royal writs, carrying the king's will to the far corners of his realm, were addressed to bishops, earls and sheriffs and the

thegns of the shire. These men were charged with the duty
of carrying out his instructions or seeing that others did
so. Bishops presided over shire courts alongside the earls
to administer justice. Through their network of thegns or
sokemen commended, that is beholden, to them as lords
or holding land on lease from bishoprics (or abbacies), the
higher clergy could call on the services of their men in
enforcing the king's will. It was thus of the first importance
to King William to secure their fealty and he made sure of
doing so when he accepted their submission to his rule.

Bishops particularly wanted to see an end to the bloodshed, the excuse always offered by those who choose to
collaborate with the enemy. To be fair, this desire was, on
the part of some clergy, quite genuine. Men of the calibre of
Bishop Wulfstan of Worcester, with his reputation for sanctity,
wanted an end to the violence. But there is a more mundane
aspect; a prime objective for an eleventh-century bishop or
abbot was to preserve the lands of his see or abbacy, and even
add to them if he could, so that they could be handed on
intact to a successor. It was a major aim of the bishops and
abbots to secure confirmation of their church's possession
of its lands. Only a king could provide such confirmation
so the vacant throne had to be filled as soon as possible. As
the victor of Hastings, William was the obvious (but not the
only) candidate and backed by a powerful army.

The king in England also controlled higher ecclesiastical preferment, a power confirmed by Pope Alexander II.
It was, therefore, vital that there be a king on the throne
able to dispense such patronage. Kings were essential to
the enforcement of reform in the Church and that would
have been in the minds of those bishops of foreign birth or
education. So clerical support for the new regime was not
entirely a matter of self-interest. Indeed, there was a theo-
logical dimension. The bishops saw William's victory as a
sign that God had favoured his cause in what was widely
seen as a trial by battle between himself and Harold.

As the *Worcester Chronicle* (D) has it; 'the French had possession of the place of slaughter, as God granted them because of the nation's sins.' A later writer, Eadmer, explained the victory as a 'miracle of God'; Norman losses in the battle had been so heavy that only God's help could explain their success.

The abbots, who, unlike the bishops, were English, took a different view. Abbot Leofric of Peterborough and Abbot Aelfwig of the New Minster, at Winchester, actually led their contingents of men into battle and other abbots had sent their men to it. There is no record of this being done by any bishop.

Laymen, too, had their own motives for co-operation. The stallers and sheriffs followed the example set by the Bishops, as did some leading thegns. The contents of the Conqueror's writs addressed to Ralph de Gael in East Anglia and Robert fitzWymarc in Essex, to Stallers (place-holders with 'seat and special duty in the king's hall') like Bondi and Eadnoth and thegns such as Wigod of Wallingford and Tofi the Proud of Somerset, are clear evidence of their readiness to obey the king. Their co-operation, with that of the bishops, ensured the submission of the population, of what may truly be called the 'occupied zone', when trouble began in the West Country and along the Welsh border before spreading to the Midlands and the North.

The motive of these men is similar to that of the bishops in that they too wished to hang on to lands and office. Many of them were to be sadly disappointed. There were other collaborators who were men of little account before the Conquest but who rose to relative prominence and prosperity under the Conqueror.

Some of the collaborators can be identified, both those who welcomed William or readily submitted, under duress or out of enlightened self-interest, and those who emerged later, the hard-faced men who did well out of the Conquest.

Archbishop Ealdred of York

Ealdred proved to be one of the Conqueror's most useful
adherents. He put his diplomatic skills, honed over several
decades, at William's disposal, organising his coronation
and ensuring the full co-operation of the other clergy
within his huge archdiocese. He used his influence in the
South as a former Bishop of Worcester. Despite Orderic
Vitalis' praise for his virtue, he had always been more of a
career diplomat than a sound diocesan bishop.

Ealdred was a Devonshire man, kinsman of his predecessor at Worcester, Lyfing. He had used the resources
of his see to resist the attacks of the Welsh and throughout Edward's reign was used as an exponent of shuttle
diplomacy in missions to the Popes, the Holy Roman
Emperor, and to Hungary to secure the return to England
of Edward the Exile, Edgar Aetheling's father. From 1060
onwards he had been Archbishop of York. It was he who
crowned both Harold and William. He died in 1069 just
as the great rebellion of that year was beginning, worn out
by his labours. In his time he had known every person of
importance in England since Cnut the Great's reign.

Giso of Wells

Leader of the 'Lotharingian Connection' (a group of ten
senior clerics prominent both before and after 1066 and
born/educated in Lotharingia, the present day Lorraine),
he supported William from the very beginning. He and his
fellow Lotharingians formed a continental fifth column in
England before the Conquest, in alliance with those bishops who were of Norman origin (of whom only William,
Bishop of London, was in office after 1066).

Giso has left his own 'memoir' of his episcopate, in which
he claims to have found his see impoverished when he
received it and to have proceeded to recover its property
unlawfully taken from it by Harold Godwinson, Archbishop
Stigand and others of their supporters. He boasts of

worming gifts of land out of King William and of persuading others to give or sell him estates. He used the proceeds to build a cloister, dormitory and refectory for his canons. His principal concern was always to enhance the endowments of his church and he advises his successors to do likewise so as to 'possess in glory the benefits of Christ's ultimate reward'. His motives for supporting William are obvious.

He had been an enemy of Harold and is full of venom towards him, accusing him of being 'puffed up with avarice' and of having robbed Wells of land at Barnwell as well as of books, vestments and sacred vessels. He was always careful to describe King Edward as King William's immediate predecessor, as though Harold had never been king. He says that Hastings had been the 'judgement of divine vengeance' on Harold. Yet King Harold had guaranteed him full jurisdiction over his lands and men 'as fully as ever he had them in King Edward's time'. We do not have Harold's side of the story. After the Conquest, Giso became part of the system through which King William controlled the West Country as his writs demonstrate.

Giso was from Saint Trond (now St Truiden) in Hesbaye in the diocese of Liege, near Maastricht. The rest of the Lotharingians are shadowy characters of whom little is known other than their general support for the Normans. The most important were; Walter, Bishop of Hereford, Queen Edith's Chaplain; Herman, Bishop of Sherborne; Leofric, Bishop of Exeter (English born but educated in Lotharingia), who acted as chancellor to King Edward, though without that exact title; Regenbald the Clerk, who acted as King William's Chancellor until 1069 when he was retired to Cirencester in considerable comfort. He had assisted William in his takeover of the services of the royal household, instructing the king, and his own successor Herfast (William's Chaplain and later Bishop of Elmham, who was the first to be officially termed Chancellor) in the workings of the English system of government.

Of the native English bishops, four were, for differing reasons, in a weak position and likely to be removed from office; they were Stigand, of course, and his brother Aethelmaer of Elmham, along with Aethelric of Selsey and Leofwine of Lichfield. They co-operated with William in the hope of retaining their bishoprics. Aethelwine of Durham co-operated at first (he was sent on a mission to King Malcolm of Scotland) but was implicated in the revolts. Siward of Rochester was overshadowed by the Archdiocese of Canterbury as his see was the smallest in England, and it fell into Norman hands shortly after Hastings.

Wulfstan of Worcester

He supported the Norman, but only after his coronation, recognising him as a validly crowned king. He used his see's resources to fend off the Welsh and proved useful later in the reign during the Revolt of the Earls in 1075. He worked in conjunction with Aethelwig, Abbot of Evesham, in ensuring that the people of his diocese accepted the new king. Pre-Conquest, he had supported Harold, again as lawfully anointed king, even journeying to Northumbria to rally the thegns to the defence of the country. After 1066 he was won over to the majority view and, in his desire to avoid further bloodshed, joined in the offer of the crown to William. His reward was that by the end of William's reign, his see, which included the 'Three Hundreds of Oswaldslaw' in Worcestershire, had become a continental-style 'liberty' from which the authority of the sheriff was excluded. He accepted the need for bishops to keep and support a company of knights, even dining with them, abstemiously in his case, and being served at table in Norman style, by pages. He died in 1095, the sole surviving Englishman in the episcopate.

The Abbots

These proved more intractable. Only two can be found fully supporting the new regime; Baldwin, Abbot of Bury

St Edmunds, who was not English, and Aethelwig of Evesham.

William's support among the abbots otherwise came from his own appointees, such as Athelhelm of Abingdon and Turold of Peterborough. Two English abbots were exiled; Aelfwold of St Benet's at Holme, who had been in charge of the defence of the eastern coast for Harold; Sihtric, Abbot of Tavistock, who 'deserted' his abbacy in 1067 to join the Sons of Harold in what the Normans called 'piracy'.

Baldwin of Bury St Edmunds

He had been King Edward's doctor and performed the same service for William. His abbacy was his reward for his services. He was born at Chartres and was a monk of St Denis Abbey but educated in Alsace. He was a member of a 'bloc' of loyal abbots appointed after the Conquest who grew rich by supporting the new king. William was to confirm him in possession of the lands and privileges of his abbey.

He used the resources of the abbey to defend East Anglia against the Danes and certainly helped to combat disorder in Norfolk after the initial surrender. He promoted the cult of St Edmund, claiming that the saint would defend his abbey, especially by giving headaches to those who attacked it. One man was driven mad in this way.

Aethelwig, Abbot of Evesham

A most useful ally for King William, promptly redeeming the lands of his abbey 'by paying the appropriate price', he served William well, rising to prominence in 1069. In that year he was given an extraordinary commission with great administrative powers. He had the authority of a royal justice over seven Midlands shires, most of western Mercia in fact, which gave him both executive and judicial powers within his '*baillia et justicia*' as the famous writ addressed to him has it. The writ was issued, probably in 1072, shortly before the campaign of King William in Scotland, and required him to see to it that all those under his command attended the king at Clarendon. He himself was to bring the five knights he owed from his abbacy also.

STALLERS, SHERIFFS AND THE ROYAL HOUSEHOLD

Most of these at this period are little more than names, but a number of them can be identified.

Ralph de Gael or 'the Staller'
He was a staller or minister of King Edward who was made earl in East Anglia shortly after the Conquest. There he was assisted by William, the Norman Bishop of London, and the royal priest Engelric, in oversight of the redemption of their lands by the English. In doing so he was guilty of a considerable degree of corruption.

Of mixed Breton/English descent he had spent much time before the Conquest on his Breton estates, earning the enmity of his Norman neighbours. His administration of his earldom was certainly irregular and Domesday Book records instances of his dealings in laying hold of estates for himself and his men without a licence from the king.

Robert fitz Wymarc
Like Earl Ralph, Robert was a Breton with land in East Anglia before 1066, at Clavering in Essex. His mother, Wymarc, was Breton and his father probably Norman. He came to William's attention before Hastings by advising him not to meet King Harold in battle as he would be overwhelmed by superior numbers. William ignored the advice but found Robert useful in the administration of Essex. The later sheriff of that shire, Swein, was Robert's son and the family held 133 hides by 1086.

Eadnoth the Staller

He had been King Edward's Steward, with lands in Dorset and Somerset. He was a royal justice and instrumental in recovering land for Wilton Abbey from the grasping hands of Earl Godwin of Wessex. He led the Somersetshire levies against the Sons of Harold and died in the skirmish which followed. His son Harding, ancestor of the fitzHardings of Bristol, also co-operated and became Portreeve of Bristol. He did well out of his service to King William after his father's death.

Of the rest, little can be done other than to name them; Bondi the Staller; Ulf Topeson of Lincoln; Eadric, Sheriff of Wiltshire and other sheriffs; Tofi of Somerset; Swawold of Oxfordshire; Northmann of Norfolk; Gamall son of Osbert in Yorkshire; and, for a time, Maerleswein, Sheriff of Lincolnshire; they all served the new king as they had served his predecessors, taking their lead from the decision of the Witan in London to submit to the Norman invader. Thus they did what office-holders have always done and what many did in Nazi-occupied Europe, even in the Channel Islands.

There was also a small but quite powerful 'French Connection', almost a Fifth Column, consisting of French, mainly Norman, friends of King Edward; Baldwin fitzHerluin, Osbern surnamed Pentecost and his nephew Alfred of Marlborough, Osbern fitzOsbern, brother of Earl William, Richard fitzRichard and Richard fitzScrob and his son Osbern fitzRichard. They held their lands mainly in Herefordshire and introduced castle building there before the Conquest. Their leader had been the king's nephew from his sister Goda, Earl Ralph of Mantes, known in England as Earl of Hereford, who died in 1057.

Others only emerged after William had taken possession of the country. They prospered in his service; men like Edward of Salisbury, known as 'the Rich', who was Sheriff of Wiltshire in the 1070s. His descendants became Earls of

Salisbury. He was one of the few Englishmen with lands of baronial extent in 1086. Colswein of Lincoln was another ministerial tenant-in-chief who built up a large holding by accumulating the estates of many lesser men who perished in the risings (J.W.F. Hill, in *Medieval Lincoln*, calls him a quisling). Aethelwig of Thetford survived the Conquest with all his estates intact and was Sheriff of Norfolk, remaining so until 1075 when he fell from grace. He was responsible for exiling Thurstin of Thetford, one of the men of St Benet at Holme. William employed a '*dapifer*' or steward called Godric as 'farmer' of confiscated estates. He was one of those who administered such lands by collecting all dues and taxes from them after offering to raise a guaranteed amount for the Treasury, and pocketing the difference if they could raise more than had to be paid to the king.

Thorkell of Arden, Sheriff of Warwickshire, also retained his lands by careful manoeuvres. His kindred channelled what wealth they had through Thorkell by becoming his tenants and holding their lands from him. Thorkell himself made allies of his Norman neighbours, like Robert d'Oilly, Robert of Stafford and William fitzAnsculf, by arranging for them to hold lands from him as his tenants, on mutually beneficial terms, and for his relatives to hold some lands under these Normans.

The overall effect of the co-operative efforts of all these men, bishops, abbots, stallers, sheriffs, royal officials of the household and rich thegns, together with their staffs and followers, was to bring about a relatively smooth transition from the government of King Harold II to that of William I and to anaesthetise the will to resist in the southern counties. It was left to the English and Anglo-Danes from north of the Humber to bring home to the Normans the real depth of English feeling and to make them fight for the rest of the country.

Epilogue

The main thrust of this book has been to demonstrate the essential truth of Sir Frank Merry Stenton's claim, in the *First Century of English Feudalism* p.148, that 'after the Battle of Hastings the chances were against the survival of the Anglo-Norman monarchy.' He rightly observed that 'the resources of the king were doubtless equal to the suppression of any purely English rising' and went on to argue that the true danger lay in the fact that the English were in touch with 'the courts of Swein Estrithson and his sons' and that the Danish kingdom was now a formidable power.

Stenton's real argument was that 'the danger of a Danish attack has received less than its due attention from historians' (mainly because it never materialised) whereas my own concern has been to show that they have equally neglected the English contribution to the problems faced by King William in the first five years after the Conquest and to show that the war against the Normans did not end at Hastings.

It has also been my purpose to rescue the reputation of Hereward, the exiled son of a prosperous king's thegn, and restore his activities to their place in the story of English Resistance to the Norman Conquest.

In presenting these arguments I have become aware of a degree of subconscious pro-Normanism in much writing about the Conquest. Perhaps historians are over impressed by the magnificence of the 'mighty works' left by the Normans; all those great cathedrals and grim castle ruins, so different in scale from the surviving Old English (usually termed 'Saxon') churches. Some accept at face value the insistence of Norman writers that the English built their halls and houses of wood. Were there, then, no stone halls? That none survive is plain, but perhaps they were not permitted to do so. According to the *Liber Eliensis*, the monastery of St Etheldreda and her church were of stone, but there is no sign of them now; that stone would certainly have been recycled in the construction of the new church and new monastic buildings.

In writing the history of any period, the historian has to use the written materials which have survived, and for the Norman period these are the charters and writs, both royal and baronial or ecclesiastical, the *Chronicles* and *Lives of Kings and Saints*, Domesday Book and its 'satellite' documents of course, all mainly the work of Anglo-Norman monks and, for the most part, in Latin (except for the *Anglo-Saxon Chronicle* and a few writs, which are in English). The monks who wrote the *Chronicles* were under the supervision of Norman Abbots and visiting Norman Bishops and, on reading them, one becomes aware of the constraints placed upon them. That version of the *Chronicle* usually referred to as (D) and from Worcester Abbey, in its entry for 1066, calls Duke William 'the Bastard', but this epithet is never found again until the writings of Orderic Vitalis in the next century. The same version tells us that Eadric 'the Wild' rose in rebellion, but not what the castlemen of Hereford had done to provoke him. 'Atrocities' by English rebels are reported; how they attacked the castles at York 'slaying many hundreds'; how Hereward and the Danes 'burnt down and devastated'

Peterborough; but their condemnation of the 'harrying of the North' is muted.

Historians, too, rather like King William, and are keen to insist that he was the only viable candidate for the throne, with the corollary that the bishops and others who threw in their lot with him had no alternative. Yet I have presented evidence that Edgar the Aetheling was seen as King Edward's heir, at first by Archbishop Ealdred and the Londoners, then by the people of the Fens and their representative as it were, Abbot Brand, and eventually by the Northumbrians, Mercians and Yorkshiremen, backed, but only up to a point, by the kings of Scotland and Denmark.

More work could surely be done to recover the history of those first five fatal years leading up to the moment when William could at last claim that he now controlled 'his newly acquired kingdom' and the full story of the English Resistance.

Maps and Genealogies

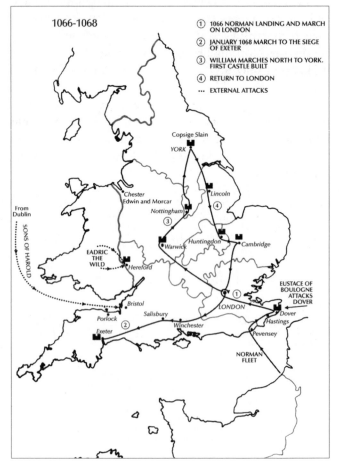

1 Map of William I's movements, 1066–8

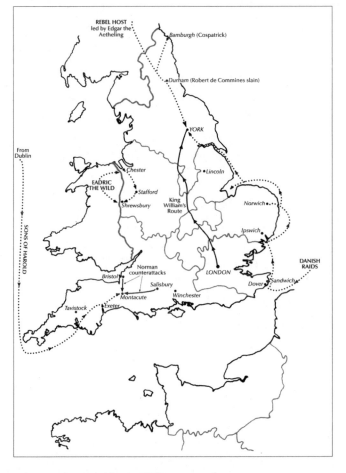

REBEL HOST
led by Edgar the
Aetheling

Bamburgh (Cospatrick)

Durham (Robert de Commines slain)

YORK

From
Dublin

Chester

Lincoln

EADRIC
THE WILD

Stafford

Shrewsbury

King
William's
Route

Norwich

SONS OF HAROLD

Ipswich

DANISH
RAIDS

Norman
counterattacks

LONDON

Bristol

Salisbury

Dover *Sandwich*

Montacute

Winchester

Tavistock *Exeter*

2 In 1069 the risings begin: William responds

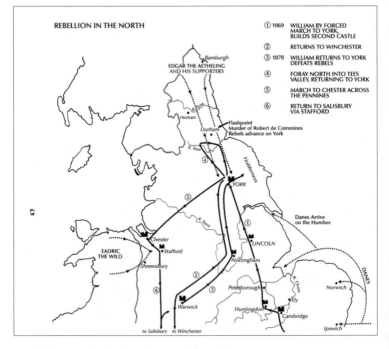

3 Rebellion in the North

4 Lincolnshire, showing lands of Hereward, Brand and Aschil

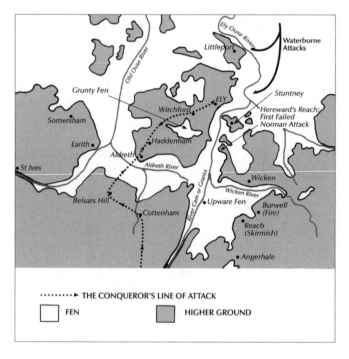

5 Maps of the attacks on Ely

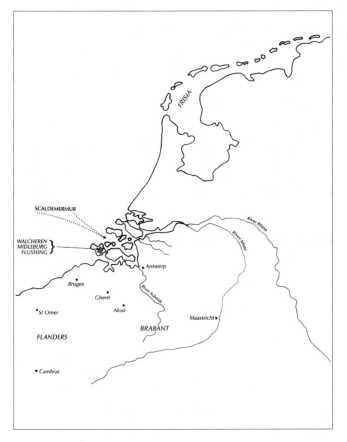

6 Location of Scaldimariland, showing the mouths of the rivers Rhine, Scheldt and Maars

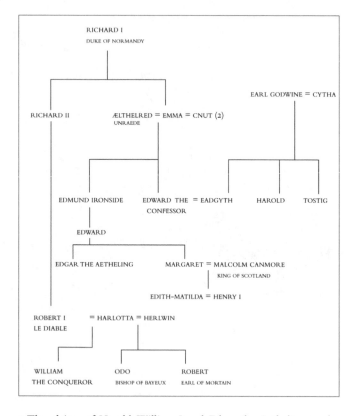

7 The claims of Harold, William I and Edgar the Aetheling to the English throne

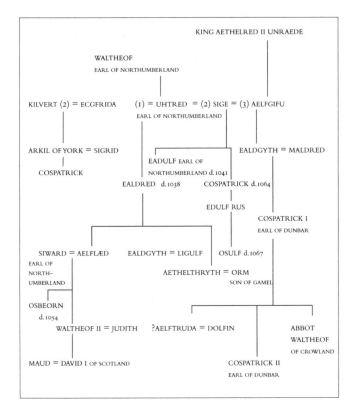

8 The House of Bamburgh

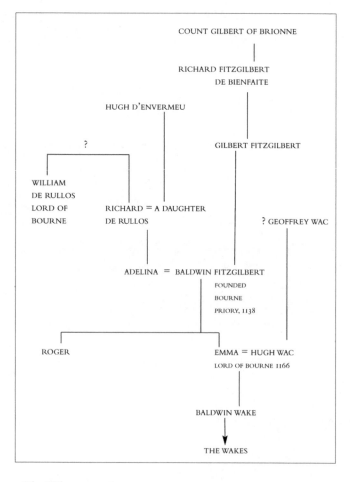

9 The Wake connection

Bibliography

PRIMARY SOURCES

Chronicles, narratives and other documentary sources

Arnold, T., 'Huntingdon, Henry of' *Historia Anglorum*. (ed.) London 1879.
—, *Simeon of Durham Opera Omnia*. (ed.) 2 Vols. R.S. London 1882,1885.
Blake, E.O. (ed.), *Liber Eliensis*, trans. by J. Fairweather (in preparation). London 1962.
Chambers, R.W., *England Before the Norman Conquest*. London, 1928.
Chibnall, M. (ed. & trans.), Ordericus Vitalis, *The Ecclesiastical History*. Oxford 1969–80.
Davis, H.W.C., *Regesta Regum Anglo-Normannorum*. Vol.1 (ed.) Oxford, 1913.
    Vol.2 (ed.) C. Johnson & H.A. Cronne, Oxford, 1956.
Douglas, D., & G.W. Greenaway, *English Historical Documents*. (ed.), London, Vol. 2 1042–1189 1953.
Foster, C.W., & T. Longley, *Lincolnshire Domesday and the Lindsey Survey*. (ed.) Lincoln Record Society, 1924.
Gaimar, Geoffrey, *L'Estoire des Engles*, (ed.) A. Bell, Anglo-Norman Text Society, Oxford, 1960.
Garmonsway, G.N., *Anglo-Saxon Chronicle*. (Trans.) London, 1953.
Hardy, T.D., & C.T. Martin, *Gesta Herewardi*. (ed.) R.S. London, 1888
—, *Hugh the Chanter, History of the Church of York*. (ed.) C. Johnson, Edinburgh, 1961.
Hunter, J., Pipe Roll 31 Henry I. (ed.) Record Commission, London, 1833.
Macray, W.D., *Chronicon Abbatiae de Evesham*. (ed.) R.S. London, 1863

Marx, J., 'Jumièges, William of', *Gesta Normannorum Ducum.* (ed.) 1914.

Maurois, André, *Le Memorial des Siècles. Onzième siècle; La Conquête de L'Angleterre par les Normandes.* (ed.) Paris, 1968.

Mellows, W.T., Hugh Candidus, *The Peterborough Chronicle,* (ed.) Oxford, 1941, incorporating the Annals of John of Peterborough.

Poitiers, William of, *Gesta Guillelmi Ducis Normannorum et Regis Anglorum.* (ed.) R. Foreville, Paris, 1952.

Robertson, A.J., (ed. & trans.) *The Laws of the Kings of England from Edmund to Henry I.* Cambridge, 1925.

Stevenson, J., *Chronicon ex Chronicis,* Florence of Worcester, (trans.) London 1853.

—, *Chronicon Monasterii de Abingdon.* (ed.) 2 Vols. R.S. London 1858.

—, *History of Crowland Abbey,* 'Ingulf'. Trans. London, 1854.

Stubbs, W., Malmesbury, William of, *Gesta Regum Anglorum.* (ed.) R.S. 1887, 1889.

—, *Select Charters* Eighth Edition. Oxford 1900.

Sturlason, Snorri, *Heimskringla; The Saga of Harald Hardrada,* (ed.) E. Monsen & A.H. Smith, Cambridge, 1932.

Williams, Ann & G.H. Martin, Domesday Book. (ed. & trans.), London, 2002.

Wilson, David M., *Bayeux Tapestry.* (ed.) British Museum, London, 1985.

SECONDARY SOURCES

Astbury, A.K., *The Black Fens.* Cambridge, 1958.

Barlow, Frank, *Edward the Confessor.* London, 1970.

—, *The English Church 1066-1154.* London, 1979.

Bartlett, R., *The Making of Europe.* London, 1993.

Bateson, E., *History of Northumberland.* Vol.I, 1893.

Bennett, Matthew, *Campaigns of the Norman Conquest.* Osprey, 2001.

—, *The Conqueror faces a fightback. History Magazine* Vol.3 No.1, Jan., 2002.

Bevis, T., *Hereward of the Fens.* Trans. *De Gestis Herewardis Saxonis.* March, 1981.

Blair, P.H., *An Introduction to Anglo-Saxon England.* Cambridge, 1956.

Brown, R.A., *Anglo-Norman Studies; Proceedings of the Battle Conferences,* Vol.1-24 1979 to 2002.

    VII. *The Norman Settlement of Herefordshire under William I.* C.Lewis, 1984.

    XIX. *Giso of Wells,* Keynes, S., 1996.

    XVIII. *The Normans as Patrons of Religious Houses 1066-1135,* 1995.

    XXI. *The Gesta Herewardi, the English and their conquerors.* H.M. Thomas, 1998.

—, *Origins of English Feudalism.* London, 1973.

Cambridgeshire and Huntingdonshire Archaeological Transactions, Vol.I

Complete Peerage, New Edition. Vol.XII Part 2.

Coss, Peter, *The Knight in Medieval England 1000-1400.* Stroud, 1996.

Darby, H.C., *Medieval Fenland.* Newton Abbot, 1949.

Davis, H.W.C., *England under the Normans and Angevins 1066-1172*. London, 1949.

De Brouard, Michel, *Guillaume le Conquérant*. Caen, 1984.

De Vries, Kelly, *The Norwegian Invasion of England in 1066*. Boydell & Boydell, 1999.

Dictionary of National Biography; Articles on Hereward, Ealdred of York and others.

Domesday Book, *England's Heritage Then and Now*. (ed.) Hinde, T., London 1985.

Douglas, D.C., *William the Conqueror*. London 1964.

Dring, W.E., *The Fenland Story*. Cambs. & Ely Educ.Comm.1967.

English Romanesque Art 1066-1200. (ed. Zarnecki, Holt & Holland). The Arts Council, London, 1984.

Farrer, C.F., *Ouse's Silent Tide*. Bedford 1921.

Fenland Notes and Queries III 1895-97.

Fowler, G., *Fenland waterways*. C.A.S. Proc. No.xxxiii 1931-2.

Freeman, E.A., *The History of the Norman Conquest of England*, 6 Vols. Oxford 1867-79.

Ganshof, F.L., *Feudalism*. London, 1961.

Gillingham, J., *Thegns and Knights in eleventh-century England; Who was then the Gentleman?* R.H. S. Trans. Sixth Series, No.V .

Green, Judith V., *The Sheriffs of William the Conqueror*. Anglo-Norman Studies 5, 1982.

Hall D., & J. Coles, *Fenland Survey*. English Heritage, 1994.

Harper, C.G., *The Cambridge, Ely and King's Lynn Road*. Chapman & Hall, 1902.

Hart, C.R., *The Danelaw; Hereward 'the Wake' and his companions*. Hambledon Press, 1992,

—, *Early Charters of Eastern England*. Leicester, 1966.

Hayward, J., *Hereward the Outlaw, Journal of Medieval History 14*. 1988.

Hayward, P., *Translation narratives in Post-Conquest Hagiography and the English Resistance to the Norman Conquest*. 1998.

Higham, N.J., *The Kingdom of Northumbria AD 350-1100*. Stroud, 1993

—, *The Death of Anglo-Saxon England*. A.Sutton, 1997.

Hill, J.W.F., *Medieval Lincoln*. Cambridge, 1948.

Hole, C., *English Folk Heroes*. Batsford, 1948.

Hooker, F.H., *The Stuntney Book*. 1984/86.

Hooper, N., *Edgar the Aetheling: Anglo-Saxon Prince, Rebel and Crusader, Anglo-Saxon England 14*. 1985.

Hudson, J., *Essential Histories; The Norman Conquest, BBC History Magazine* Vol.4 No. 1 Jan, 2003.

Jerrold, D., *An Introduction to the History of England*. London, 1949.

Jewell, H., *English Local Administration in the Middle Ages*. Newton Abbot, 1972.

John, Eric, *Reassessing Anglo-Saxon England*. Manchester University Press, 1996.

Johnson-Smith, T., *The Norman Conquest of Durham*. Haskins Soc. Journ. 4, 1994.

Kapelle, W.E., *The Norman Conquest of the North*. London, 1979.

King, Edmund,*Peterborough Abbey 1086-1310*. Cambridge, 1973.

Lethbridge, T.C., *Articles in Proc. C.A.S.* 1931, 1934, 1935.

Lyons, D., & S., *Magna Brittania*. Cambridgeshire, 1808.

Maitland, F.W., *Domesday Book and Beyond*. Cambridge, 1907.

Matthew, D.J.A., *The Norman Conquest*. London, 1966.

McLynn, Frank, *1066 The Year of the Three Battles*. London, 1999.

Miller, E., *The Abbey and Bishopric of Ely*. Cambridge, 1951.

Oman, Sir Charles, *England Before the Norman Conquest*. London, 1921.

Pollock, F., & F.W. Maitland, *The History of English law before the time of Edward I*. Cambridge, 1968.

Poole, A.L., *From Domesday Book to Magna Carta 1087-1216*. Oxford, 1961.

Prestwich, J.O., *Anglo-Norman Feudalism and the Problem of Continuity; Past and Present No.26,* 1963.

Prestwich, M., *Miles in Armis Strenuus; the Knight at War*, R.H.S. Trans. Sixth Series, No.V.

Roffe, D., *From Thegnage to Barony: Sake and Soke, Title and Tenants-in-Chief.* XII. 1989.

Round, J.H., *Feudal England*, London, 1909 *Peerage and Pedigree. Studies in Peerage and Family History*.

Sayles, G.O., *The medieval Foundations of England*. London, 1948.

Scientific Survey of the Cambridge District. B.A.A.S., 1938.

Stafford, Pauline, *Unification and Conquest; a political and social history of England in the tenth and eleventh centuries*. London, 1989.

Stenton, Doris, (ed.) *Preparatory to Anglo-Saxon England*.

Stenton, F.M., *Anglo-Saxon England*, Oxford, 1971. *First Century of English Feudalism 1066-1166*. Oxford 1932. *Presidential Address to R.H.S. Series IV No. xxvi* 1944.

Taylor, Alison, *Anglo-Saxon Cambridgeshire*. Cambridge, 1978.

Tilbrook, R., & C.V. Roberts, *Norfolk's Churches, Great and Small*. Norwich, 1997.

Van Houts, Elisabeth, *Hereward and Flanders, Anglo-Saxon England No.28*, 1999.

Victoria County History:

    Bedfordshire Vol.I

    Cambridgeshire Vol.I

    Herefordshire Vol.I

    Huntingdon Vol.I.

    Norfolk Vol.I.

Walker, I., *Harold, the Last Anglo-Saxon King*. A.Sutton, 1997.

Wedgewood, Iris, *Fenland Rivers*. Rich & Cowan, 1936.

Williams, Ann, *The English and the Norman Conquest*. Woodbridge, 1995.

Wood, M., *Domesday. BBC Classics*, 1999.

List of Illustrations

Index

TEMPUS – REVEALING HISTORY

Britannia's Empire
A Short History of the British Empire
BILL NASSON

'Crisp, economical and witty' *TLS*
'An excellent introduction the subject' *THES*

£12.99   0 7524 3808 5

Born to be Gay
A History of Homosexuality
WILLIAM NAPHY

'Fascinating' *The Financial Times*
'Excellent' *Gay Times*

£9.99   0 7524 3694 5

Madmen
A Social History of Madhouses,
Mad-Doctors & Lunatics
ROY PORTER

'Fascinating'
The Observer

£12.99   0 7524 3730 5

William II
Rufus, the Red King
EMMA MASON

'A thoroughly new reappraisal of a much
maligned king. The dramatic story of his life is
told with great pace and insight'
John Gillingham

£25   0 7524 3528 0

To Kill Rasputin
The Life and Death of Grigori Rasputin
ANDREW COOK

'Andrew Cook is a brilliant investigative historian'
Andrew Roberts
'Astonishing' *The Daily Mail*

£9.99   0 7524 3906 5

Private 12768
Memoir of a Tommy
JOHN JACKSON
FOREWORD BY HEW STRACHAN

'A refreshing new perspective' *The Sunday Times*
'At last we have John Jackson's intensely
personal and heartfelt little book to remind us
there was a view of the Great War other than
Wilfred Owen's' *The Daily Mail*

£9.99   0 7524 3531 0

The Unwritten Order
Hitler's Role in the Final Solution
PETER LONGERICH

'Compelling' *Richard Evans*
'The finest account to date of the many twists
and turns in Adolf Hitler's anti-semitic obsession'
Richard Overy

£12.99   0 7524 3328 8

The Vikings
MAGNUS MAGNUSSON

'Serious, engaging history'
BBC History Magazine

£9.99   0 7524 2699 0

If you are interested in purchasing other books published by Tempus, or in case you have difficulty finding any
Tempus books in your local bookshop, you can also place orders directly through our website

www.tempus-publishing.com

TEMPUS – REVEALING HISTORY

D-Day The First 72 Hours
WILLIAM F. BUCKINGHAM

'A compelling narrative' *The Observer*

A *BBC History Magazine* Book of the Year 2004

£9.99   0 7524 2842 X

The London Monster
Terror on the Streets in 1790
JAN BONDESON

'Gripping' *The Guardian*

'Excellent... monster-mania brought a reign of terror to the ill-lit streets of the capital' *The Independent*

£9.99   0 7524 3327 X

London
A Historical Companion
KENNETH PANTON

'A readable and reliable work of reference that deserves a place on every Londoner's bookshelf' *Stephen Inwood*

£20   0 7524 3434 9

M: MI5's First Spymaster
ANDREW COOK

'Serious spook history' *Andrew Roberts*

'Groundbreaking' *The Sunday Telegraph*

'Brilliantly researched' *Dame Stella Rimington*

£20   0 7524 2896 9

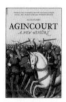

Agincourt A New History
ANNE CURRY

'A highly distinguished and convincing account' *Christopher Hibbert*

'A *tour de force*' *Alison Weir*

'*The* book on the battle' *Richard Holmes*

A *BBC History Magazine* Book of the Year 2005

£25   0 7524 2828 4

Battle of the Atlantic
MARC MILNER

'The most comprehensive short survey of the U-boat battles' *Sir John Keegan*

'Some events are fortunate in their historian, none more so than the Battle of the Atlantic. Marc Milner is *the* historian of the Atlantic campaign... a compelling narrative' *Andrew Lambert*

£12.99   0 7524 3332 6

The English Resistance
The Underground War Against the Normans
PETER REX

'An invaluable rehabilitation of an ignored resistance movement' *The Sunday Times*

'Peter Rex's scholarship is remarkable' *The Sunday Express*

£12.99   0 7524 3733 X

Elizabeth Wydeville: The Slandered Queen
ARLENE OKERLUND

'A penetrating, thorough and wholly convincing vindication of this unlucky queen' *Sarah Gristwood*

'A gripping tale of lust, loss and tragedy' *Alison Weir*

A *BBC History Magazine* Book of the Year 2005

£18.99   0 7524 3384 9

If you are interested in purchasing other books published by Tempus, or in case you have difficulty finding any Tempus books in your local bookshop, you can also place orders directly through our website

www.tempus-publishing.com

TEMPUS – REVEALING HISTORY

Quacks Fakers and Charlatans in Medicine
ROY PORTER

'A delightful book' *The Daily Telegraph*
'Hugely entertaining' *BBC History Magazine*

£12.99   0 7524 2590 0

The Tudors
RICHARD REX

'Up-to-date, readable and reliable. The best introduction to England's most important dynasty' *David Starkey*
'Vivid, entertaining... quite simply the best short introduction' *Eamon Duffy*
'Told with enviable narrative skill... a delight for any reader' *THES*

£9.99   0 7524 3333 4

The Kings & Queens of England
MARK ORMROD

'Of the numerous books on the kings and queens of England, this is the best'
Alison Weir

£9.99   0 7524 2598 6

The Covent Garden Ladies
Pimp General Jack & the Extraordinary Story of Harris's List
HALLIE RUBENHOLD

'Sex toys, porn... forget Ann Summers, Miss Love was at it 250 years ago' *The Times*
'Compelling' *The Independent on Sunday*
'Marvellous' *Leonie Frieda*
'Filthy' *The Guardian*

£9.99   0 7524 3739 9

 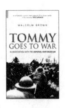

Okinawa 1945
GEORGE FEIFER

'A great book... Feifer's account of the three sides and their experiences far surpasses most books about war'
Stephen Ambrose

£17.99   0 7524 3324 5

Tommy Goes To War
MALCOLM BROWN

'A remarkably vivid and frank account of the British soldier in the trenches'
Max Arthur
'The fury, fear, mud, blood, boredom and bravery that made up life on the Western Front are vividly presented and illustrated'
The Sunday Telegraph

£12.99   0 7524 2980 4

Ace of Spies The True Story of Sidney Reilly
ANDREW COOK

'The most definitive biography of the spying ace yet written... both a compelling narrative and a myth-shattering *tour de force*'
Simon Sebag Montefiore
'The absolute last word on the subject' *Nigel West*
'Makes poor 007 look like a bit of a wuss'
The Mail on Sunday

£12.99   0 7524 2959 0

Sex Crimes
From Renaissance to Enlightenment
W.M. NAPHY

'Wonderfully scandalous'
Diarmaid MacCulloch

£10.99   0 7524 2977 9

If you are interested in purchasing other books published by Tempus, or in case you have difficulty finding any Tempus books in your local bookshop, you can also place orders directly through our website

www.tempus-publishing.com